THE LOST SUPPER

Reawakening Communion's Power to Guide Us Through Life's Storms

Michael Wolff

AuthorHouse™
1663 Liberty Drive
Bloomington, IN 47403
www.authorhouse.com
Phone: 1-800-839-8640

©2009 Michael Wolff. All rights reserved.

No part of this book may be reproduced, stored in a retrieval system, or transmitted by any means without the written permission of the author.

First published by AuthorHouse 11/11/2009

ISBN: 978-1-4259-2015-9 (e)
ISBN: 978-1-4259-2047-0 (sc)

Library of Congress Control Number: 2006902521

Printed in the United States of America
Bloomington, Indiana

This book is printed on acid-free paper.

All scripture quotations in "The Lost Supper" are from the New American Standard translation and used via special permission (July, 2004) from the Lockman Foundation, to wit:
Scripture quotations taken from the New American Standard Bible®, Copyright © 1960, 1962, 1963, 1968, 1971, 1972, 1973, 1975, 1977, 1995 by The Lockman Foundation
Used by permission. (www.Lockman.org)

All definitions of Hebrew and Greek words are taken from Strong's Exhaustive Concordance, (1980, Abingdon Press, and PC Study Bible for same (1995, Biblesoft)

To my wife Tammi, for all of the personal sacrifice she has made, and her steadfast love and support through my struggles necessary to make this book possible.

To Cec Murphey, for his steadfast financial and prayer support, and unmerited love that has been key to getting *Reconnections Ministries* off the ground and making this book possible.

To Michael Wells, for constantly reminding me of what a true disciple of Christ looks like, what the true church should look like, what God is doing around the world, and for the constant source of wisdom that only a disciple's lifestyle can yield.

To David Manuel, for encouraging me and being a beacon of light and hope in my darkest hour.

To John Calea, for being an example of what one man truly sold out to God can do in this world.

"The Lost Supper" is the property of Michael S. Wolff. It is not to be copied or reproduced in any way without the express written consent of Michael S. Wolff. If this copy is electronically transferred one copy only may be printed by the recipient for private use only, and the file may not be forwarded or electronically transferred to any other recipient without the express written consent of Michael S. Wolff, and then only for the personal use of said recipient.

Michael may be contacted via email at readywriter99@yahoo.com

TABLE OF CONTENTS

I. What to do With Life's Storms? 1

II. Whatever Happened to the Passover? 7

III. A Love to Embrace, An Admonishment to Consider 24

IV. Ministering and Experiencing Admonishment 35

V. Prodigals, Fathers, and Brothers 49

VI. To Unbelievers and Believers 61

VII. Recognizing Sin 70

VIII. The Soma: the Body of Christ 81

IX: The Matthew 5 Alternative 91

X. The Best Confession 104

XI. Prayer and Confession: The Process 118

XII. Et tu, Judas? 138

XIII. Walking Through a Powerful Ceremony 146

XIV. A Few Final Considerations.. 159

XV. Bringing it Back to the Church.. 166

XVI. It's up to You Now... 178

I. WHAT TO DO WITH LIFE'S STORMS?

Life is full of storms. Sometimes these tempests are thrust upon us, and sometimes we create them ourselves out of our natural worldly desires. Regardless, the certainty remains that fallen beings create storms in life. Given these squalls are inevitable, we are left with two choices as to what to do when the clouds begin to gather, and toss about our formerly serene seas: 1) let them sink us, or, 2) learn how to pilot our ships deftly through them to safety. The storms of life aren't the issue, as much as what we do with them and what sort of people that leads us to become in the end.

The effects of our storms can be temporary and treatable, and the collateral damage light, if we learn how to navigate through them with integrity and purpose. However, they can also become insurmountable if we allow them to overwhelm us by refusing to confront them. At that point *they* become the navigators of life, and we become hapless spectators. When we rationalize and cover up our indiscretions, we allow small squalls to turn into raging gales. The key to piloting our ships through these storms effectively is to acknowledge they exist, keep our eyes upon Jesus, the Lighthouse of our faith, and with Him maintain a steady and consistent course. That means employing every tool from the abundant supply we have been given to combat the enemies of our faith. As long as we keep the prow headed directly into the wind and waves, they may rock us, but they will not capsize us. If we let go of our rudder, though, and let our circumstances control our direction, they will have their way with us. That almost always leads to shipwreck.

Sadly, we have made an art form of vainly trying to dodge the storms by rationalizing sin in the modern church, rather than confronting it. We have become far more interested in appearances than substance, and far more interested in maintaining comfort than confronting truth. We ignore or rationalize away the warning signs, because we need to maintain the appearance of well-being we have created for ourselves. When we do, the prows of our ships turn away from the winds, and the payment becomes far greater. Failure to address our storms causes us to lose control over the inevitable consequences of our indiscretions, and become driven by them into ever-deeper waters. We allow the façade we've created to pilot the ship, and no longer use the rudder God has given us to steer through it. Sooner or later, the Piper must be paid.

If we ignore the Spirit's call to deal with our issues over an extended period of time, temporary slip-ups become dangerous practices. These then yield stifling addictions, with all of their inevitable collateral damage. We become lost in a sea of rationalization and denial, and can develop into the worst sort of hypocrites. We proclaim one truth, while living in an entirely different reality. It is this very thing that the unbelieving sit back and mock, as they witness instances of divorce, substance addiction, deceptive business practice, and worldliness in the church paralleling those in the world today. Knowing we're slipping under the waves, and yet feeling powerless to do anything about it, either capsizes us or something within awakens and cries out for help. We realize we've lost our course, and therefore are incapable of finding our way out alone. We know that without the sure hand of God, and the help of the fellowship to restore our course, we will end up shipwrecked.

Leaving the Church to Find Help?

Ever increasing numbers of the faithful caught up in these circumstances pass by churches on their way to 12-step programs and Christian therapists every day. They're trying to find the help they seek. They desire places where they can confess the habitual patterns of sin that now control them to others who can come to their aid. It is now common practice for churches to refer out their emotionally troubled and addicted members, because they believe they have nothing to offer that competes effectively with these programs. Is this what God wants, His people *leaving* the church in search of emotional healing? Is God so short-sighted that He

> **Is this what God wants? His people *leaving* the church in search of emotional healing?**

failed to provide a biblical, practical healing program for His people in any day or culture?

He has provided! God knows we are going to sin, and therefore gives us ways to make it through life's storms without despairing *(1 Cor. 10:13)*. The various 12-step programs that so many in the church now flock to—the ones that have helped thousands to overcome their addictions—are identical in theory and practice to the ceremony God gave specifically for the emotional and spiritual well-being of His people: Communion. Yes, I said *Communion*. We have just abandoned its biblical practice, and been abandoned in turn by its power.

Early in my walk of faith, I began to wonder why a ceremony that seemed to hold the power of health, life, and even death in the early church had been reduced to fifteen minute rituals sandwiched in to the end of church services once a month. Like a good churchgoer, up until that time I just went through the motions of Communion without truly understanding its meaning, its purpose, or the power it held. I kept looking for something transforming in the way it was done, but to no avail. I walked away from traditional ceremonies feeling no different than I did when I walked in. I noticed the same reaction from most of those around me. Something within called me to find a deeper meaning than the one I had come to expect from my prior experiences.

I threw out all of my traditional understandings, and re-examined the Passover of the Exodus, the actions and words of Jesus at His last Passover, the practices of the Pentecostal Church in Acts, and the instructions of Paul in 1st Corinthians. I came to find that Communion was a ceremony that was full of power to maintain a state of emotional and spiritual well-being. However, those who wanted to find its power had to come to seek more than just its comforts. They would also have to be willing to accept its challenges.

When biblically observed, Communion becomes God's lighthouse in our stormy nights. It brings to the surface all manners of buried sin and suffering, gives us a forum to confront them and neuter their power, attacks the disease of superficiality the American church now struggles with, provides hope for a brighter tomorrow, and brings together fellowships in a bond of unity like no other single process available. As I put what I learned into practice with a few other brave souls willing to enter in to this trial-by-fire, lives were transformed before our eyes.

Sin addictions that had held people under their control for years were confronted and confessed. The fellowship came together to pray, and to do the work of repentance and cleansing. God revealed Himself through it all, and liberated those who blessed Him through honoring the reason for His Table.

The Table Full of Grace *and* Truth

Why isn't the church gleaning these benefits? We don't take a balanced approach to Communion. In John 1, Jesus is described as the living Word of God that came to us in the flesh: full of grace *and* truth. Any person who encountered Jesus experienced both the warmth of the grace that was His love, and the sting of the truth that was His admonishment. They came away understanding the abundant comforts of His merciful embrace, but at the same time had to confront the unnerving challenges presented by His words of correction and command. In the modern church, we have ignored half of this equation, and made Communion singularly about grace. We've set aside the admonishments and commands, because they're messy and inconvenient. But they, too, are a vital part of the rudder God has provided to navigate life's stormy seas. The Jesus that presides over today's ceremonies has become an idol full of grace *only*, not the holy and righteous and just God full of grace *and* truth.

The biblical Communion message is certainly, "Do this in remembrance of Me." We come to indeed remember the price He paid at Calvary to show mercy to the world He was sent to save. Yet the message is also, and equally, "Examine yourself," with dire forewarnings of judgment if partaken of unworthily. It is because we now largely ignore the critical aspect of self-examination through large group participation with little instruction, a few minutes for prayer, and no confession and interaction with others, that something powerful is lost. When we ignore the balance that roots out covered-up sin, and seek only the love without the correction—when we make Communion about nothing but grace—there is no healing because we strip it of its teeth. Jesus' grace *without* Jesus' truth has led us into the malaise we now witness in modern American Christianity.

The Corinthians made Communion into a social gathering, refusing the command for self-examination, and it led to physical *weakness, sickness, and death (1 Cor. 11:30)*. They dishonored the Lord's Table with their superficial observances, and it cost them dearly. Sadly, the majority of today's churches do the very same thing, with the very same results. They don't tap into the emotional and spiritual healing Communion was ordained to maintain. The result is the harvesting of superficiality and hypocrisy in the body of Christ.

Too many of our members "eat and drink judgment upon themselves," by partaking when they have not considered their condition very carefully. Unlike our church leaders, 12-step ministers and therapists have figured out that love without admonishment accomplishes little in the way of true renewal of mind and spirit. They've learned it's about honesty, and deeds and actions of repentance, as well as grace. This is why the emotionally troubled in the church flock to them, and now see her as little more than a place of gathering on Sundays to listen to a sermon and sing a few songs. If we'll learn from those our emotionally troubled are flocking to, restore the balance of grace and truth to Communion, and put it back into the biblical environment of intimate spiritual family, we can reawaken true addiction recovery and healing within the church.

The Spiking Event of Fellowship

Robert Lewis wrote a book about the masculine journeys he and two of his friends embarked upon while raising their sons. In *Raising a Modern-Day Knight,* he talks about *spiking* events. These are events that are the culminating and sealing acts of a journey that has taken considerable time and effort to complete. They are the crowning glory of struggles of endurance that proclaim arrival at the finish line. They herald the culmination of a journey of faith, hope, and love that forever and indelibly leave their mark on us. We've been through the valleys, climbed the mountains, and arrived at the summit! Lewis relates these journeys to the three primary shots in a volleyball game, the final one being the *spike*.

> The spike is an aggressive, powerful play. When a player rises to the net and spikes the ball into the other court, he puts an exclamation point on his team's execution. A good spike finalizes everything his team has worked

so hard to accomplish. A ceremony is like the spike. It drives home the point with unmistakable certainty.[1]

God's ultimate gift to the small-group fellowship—the ceremony, the exclamation point—is Communion! It is the *spike* that drives home the bond of unity and healing in the fellowship of believers with unmistakable certainty. It was the

> **Communion is God's "spike" that leads to the healing and bonding of His people.**

culminating event of Jesus' ministry on earth with His disciples. His Passover was their final debriefing, and His grand epitaph to all He had shown and taught them. Communion is God's aggressive, powerful play that drives out superficiality, opens doors to healing, and cements the bonds of unity that are the stuff small-group fellowships should be made of.

If we would apply the balm of Communion to our emotional and spiritual wounds, we would see the stream of the hurting who now flow out of the church begin to stream back in. By putting into practice the principles in this book, emotional healing and stability can be brought back within the confines of fellowship, and removed from the offices of *the professionals*. All we need to do is reawaken our eyes now heavy with sleep to a gift that has always been there for us! Through the regular practice of the ceremony God gave His people to facilitate repentance, confession, and intimate fellowship we can navigate the squalls of life in the Spirit of God, so they don't become raging gales that capsize us.

Of all the moments He shared with His disciples—of all miracles performed and lessons taught—Jesus said exclusively of His Passover, "I have *earnestly desired* to do this with you" *(Luke 22:15)*. If you will read on, you will discover why He still longs to join us at His Table of truth and grace, and through a balance of love and correction guide our frail ships deftly through the storms of life and on to safe harbor!

II. WHATEVER HAPPENED TO THE PASSOVER?

Your name is Thaddaeus, you're one of the twelve, and you've been a part of a great adventure with this itinerant preacher for the past three years. While surprises have become a part of life with this Jesus, you've settled into somewhat of a routine. You and the other disciples have spent your time watching everything from the mundane to the unreal develop through His ministry. You have been constantly sent out to preach His message, and then brought back to His side to discuss your experiences. You've seen the dead raised, the sick healed, water turned to wine, and amazing numbers of people fed to overflowing with one child's basket of food. You've also seen Him talk quietly with prostitutes, tax collectors, and minister to a wide variety of the most messed-up people no one else would give a chance.

However, ever since His arrival in Jerusalem the ride has been as unstable as a moneychanger's table in the Temple courts. You and the other disciples cheered in joyous jubilation as He rode triumphantly into the city, but ever since then this Messiah has seemed on an unrelenting collision course with the religious leaders. The Scribes and Pharisees test Him, and pepper Him with trick questions designed to trap Him, and further their own purposes. He counters them with a defiance, authority, and wisdom that has left them emotionally unnerved, theologically undressed, and growing more hostile by the day.

It seems Jesus' mood has changed from loving to overtly combative, as with every passing moment, and every authoritative word coming from His lips, He moves closer and closer to some master plan that you and the others remain totally clueless about. Just recently the tensions boiled over, as Jesus was confronted by His robed irritants after healing a blind man at the Pool of Siloam. He delivered an angry and stinging rebuke: calling them hypocrites, whitewashed tombs, and a brood of vipers. This One you had come to know as an extraordinary man of peace and love seems somehow antsy and irritable. His face is set like flint towards a gauntlet that He must run, but one nonetheless that unnerves and upsets Him. You have this uneasy feeling that what began in triumph is going to end in a no-holds-barred wrestling match for the hearts and minds of the people of Israel. You have the unnerving feeling you're going to get caught at ground zero.

The Passover is at hand, and all Jerusalem is in preparation for the holy ceremony. One of your brothers asks Jesus what He intends to do to celebrate it. In response, He tells two of your fellow disciples to go find a certain man in the city and tell him that He has need of a large room the man owns. They are then to go with him to prepare for the meal. The two leave on their errand, and some time later Jesus leads the rest of you to an upper room at the man's house where you will all partake. His mood is somber, and the joy you have come to know this Jesus for has been replaced by a sense of fervent purpose and total dedication to this cause that has so captured His thoughts of late.

When all are finally seated He says something that takes you aback—not that it's earth-shattering in its message, but you've never heard Him say it before of any of the amazing events you have all participated in together. Jesus, with eyes full of intense destiny, says, "I have earnestly desired to eat this Passover with you before I suffer. For I say to you, I shall never again eat it until it is fulfilled in the kingdom of God" *(Luke 22:16)*. He has never, through this incredible journey over the past three years, relayed to you and the others an earnest desire to do something with you. He has just gone and done it. Though He had spoken many times about suffering at the hands of the Jews, somehow now you know that it's imminent. The die is about to be cast. You cast a glance, first Peter's way and then John's, thinking surely these two favorites of Jesus would understand what all of this means. You find them blankly staring back at you and the others as if to say, "Don't ask us!"

Jesus then says something even more unsettling: "Truly, I say to you that one of you will betray Me!" You respond reflexively, "Surely it's not I, this betrayer you speak of?" The others all anxiously ponder the same question, rocked by this revelation. Jesus casts a quick, penetrating stare around the room and continues, "The Son of Man is to go just as it is written of Him, but woe to that man by whom the Son of Man is betrayed! It would have been good for that man if he had not been born." Uneasiness has now turned to sheer panic as you and your brothers look anxiously about you, all wondering who this traitor could possibly be. Then Judas speaks up: "Surely it is not I, Rabbi?" This draws a terse response from Jesus: "You have said it yourself." You don't know why, but Jesus then speaks another mystery to Judas: "What you do, do quickly."

A look you have never seen before comes over the face of Judas, and you know that somehow he knows exactly what Jesus meant. He leaves the room for some unknown reason, but again you have a sense that everything happening on this night will be a part of this destination Jesus seems intent on pursuing to its ultimate conclusion. Somehow you and the others are beginning to see that the end isn't going to be a particularly happy one.

The next act of Jesus doesn't do anything to calm your nerves. He takes a washbowl and begins to wash Peter's feet. Peter, now sharing the concern felt round the table, fumbles for the right words to say—anything to soothe the mood of the moment that has become more unnerving with every tick of the clock. So he ventures into the perilous mood of the evening and carries on a conversation with Jesus that earns him a rebuke. It has become clear that this is no night for small talk, questioning, or verbal banter of any kind. As you have sensed something coming for days, now it becomes dauntingly clear. Whatever this mission Jesus is on it will be fulfilled, and soon. You and your brothers seem to just be along for the ride. You all sense that before this night is done terrible things are going to happen, and there is not a thing you, Peter, John, James, or any of the rest can do about it. This is a night to listen, watch, and wait for the Master to say or do whatever it is that He seems so set upon doing. It is a night, for better or worse, that none of you will ever forget.

A One-of-a-Kind Event

Jesus didn't say it when He preached the Sermon on the Mount. He didn't say it when He raised Lazarus from the dead, fed the five thousand, or rode into Jerusalem to thunderous praise. Yet of this one event, He told His disciples, "I have *earnestly desired* to do this with you." The Passover had begun in Israel. Jesus had formed intimate bonds with His hand-selected followers and, in His moment of distress, His moment of need, more than anything else He wanted to celebrate the Passover with them. Those who heard in parables would have to wait. Those who followed, and yet refused to commit fully, would have the door to the upper room closed to them. This was a night of preparation, both for Jesus and His hand-selected apprentices about to be cast into trial by fire. It was an event that would carry on its shoulders both the fate of His disciples and His message into history. This was to be a night like none other.

I believe the reason for this desire was the life-giving teaching and example He wanted to set before them as His last act on earth. He was about to hand the baton of ministry to His church of twelve, for they were about to carry His message forward into history. This was to be the final briefing for His new cornerstones. As we witness the passion of this moment, Jesus' last act on the eve of the most important event in all of history, we must ask ourselves what has made it the relatively tame and non-threatening ritual it has become today.

> **We must ask ourselves what has made Communion the relatively tame and non-threatening ritual it has become today.**

So important was Communion that it was one of only two ceremonies ordained by God in the New Testament. The first was baptism: the New Testament equivalent of Old Testament circumcision. This symbolized the public celebration of God's gift of atonement. The other is Communion, which finds its roots in the accounts of Christ's partaking of the Old Testament Passover meal with his disciples. It is the celebration of our sanctification, and therefore given to us to be done regularly, to ensure the ongoing maintenance and maturity of the process of faith once begun at baptism.

As a young seeker, I witnessed many Communions come and go that seemed strangely insignificant to me. I began to wonder how a ceremony that had come to carry the power of sickness, and even death, could have become something that carried such an air of normalcy. I must assume the Holy Spirit led me to these questions because I, like most people, had come to accept modern church observances as one of those rituals you just did without giving it much thought. However, when I began to read the accounts and teachings in the Bible of Paul's message in 1st Corinthians, along with the Communion story of Jesus at the Passover with His disciples, it became evident that God placed *quite* an importance on it.

I began to search the scriptures, and experiment with different ways to make the Communion Table more closely emulate the biblical accounts of Jesus and Paul with a group of teens I was discipling at the time. We studied, prayed, experimented, and watched for God to do one of those *new things* He said He was always about. Through our studies and experimentation, God revealed a method of fully experiencing His Table that is at the same time a great comfort in the love of Jesus there to embrace, and a gauntlet thrown down through His admonishments we must there consider. Given proper time, placed in the proper setting, and observed with the proper reverence and understanding, Communion fills our inner desire to gain freedom from sinful practices that hold us in bondage to our flesh. It teaches us the true meaning of costly grace, and keeps our emotions and spirit in a state of readiness for the minefields living life as redeemed sinners always impose.

The word *Communion* comes from the Latin, "communis," and the Greek, "koin:" which mean to have something shared by everyone who participates together in fellowship. The relationship inferred here far exceeds mere association. Through years of the church disseminating knowledge without requiring participation, the modern Communion experience has lost the vital part of *fellowship more than association*. We sit in church on Sunday while the pastor and elders hand out the Elements. The pastor then prays, and the musicians play one of our favorite Communion songs. We then pray for a few minutes, as perhaps an invitation is given to ask God for the forgiveness of sins. Paul's 1st Corinthians Communion instructions are perhaps read, but if they are they typically cut off at, "Do this in remembrance of Me." Rarely are the verses beyond that which deal with the uncomfortable part of the ceremony even read, much less explained or taught. Then the Elements are partaken of. While this is all done in a well-meaning manner, to most it has become but ritual without much reflection.

Psychologist, Dr. Larry Crabb, describes the modern Communion observance in his breakthrough book *Connecting*:

Protestants have tended to devalue and mostly abandon the practice of formal confession. A few moments once a month of private self-examination before receiving Communion, for many a token and not terribly upsetting look at themselves, is about all that's left. 2

The Missing Element

The self-examination of which Paul speaks in 1st Corinthians—the part typically ignored in the church today—is that part of Communion that we need to take fuller advantage of to glean the fruit of a rich ceremony. It is the very part where participation in the body that so far exceeds mere association occurs. The power of Communion is found in taking seriously the admonishment to examine ourselves, as much as it is in understanding the grace provided through Christ's sacrifice. When Crabb says that confession of sin has become *private, token, and not terribly upsetting* within the confines of Communion, he speaks to the lack of understanding its admonishments. When you remove half of any recipe, you don't end up with what was intended. People don't typically enjoy the finished product, because it doesn't taste like the real thing.

Jesus said of Communion that His flesh was real food, and that His blood was real drink. He claimed that whoever ate that flesh and drank that blood would remain in Him, and that He would be in them as well *(John 6:55)*. This tells us two things: 1) Communion is an impactful and binding event, much more than a mere symbolic acknowledgement of grace in our lives. His flesh and blood are to affect us in tangible, lasting ways, and, 2) those who partake in this food remain in Him, and He in them. The word *remain* is the same word we find in His teaching in John 15, where He instructs us to bear fruit that *remains*. It is the word that He also uses when, in that same chapter, He calls us repeatedly to abide [remain] in Him.

Jesus wants us to be in a continual process of being and bearing fruit that will last a lifetime. This process is referred to as *sanctification*. Communion exists to regularly perfect what begins at conversion through the process of sanctification. While it is solely grace that saves us, it is more than just grace that sanctifies us—and more than grace alone that leads us to a fulfilling Communion experience. It is the combination of the grace *and* truth that Jesus was. The *truth* part of the equation always causes chaos and hurt as it does its sanctifying work, just as the commands Jesus *requires* of us always cause discomfort. Yet it is vital chaos and vital hurt, and sanctification is but a myth without it.

The definition of *sanctification* [hagiasmos] is to fulfill, or complete, the process of purification. It is a process that effects both the heart and the lifestyle of a person. Sanctification is the lifelong pursuit of Christ *by* the disciple, coupled with the lifelong work of the Holy Spirit *in* the disciple. It fulfills, perfects, and completes what God begins as a sovereign work of grace. A true Communion experience must include equal measures of mercy and admonition, as Jesus' conduct towards everyone He touched so abundantly demonstrates.

When the *command* to examine ourselves is approached with sincere humility and a desire to mature, Communion can and should be unnerving, because it reveals with intense light the sin which indwells all of us. Whenever we sincerely ask God to search our hearts, try our thoughts,

> **We must understand that The Lost Supper is about more than just grace—much, much more.**

and reveal any sinful ways we may be thinking or living in *(Ps. 139:23)* as David did, we open up Pandora's Box. It is a box filled with conflict and insecurity. God will bring to our remembrance any of a number of things we have shoved into the deep recesses in our minds through rationalization and denial. But *we* must do the asking. God cannot and will not force conviction upon the soul that has become numb to His promptings. The healing made available to us through Communion must begin with this journey into the darkness of our flesh, if we want to experience true light of grace.

Thus, we must understand that *The Lost Supper* is about more than just grace—much, much more! The missing element to modern day Communion observances is simply our refusal to open the door to the necessary chaos that will result in healing. The writer of Hebrews would call it refusing the discipline that, were we to embrace it, would bring about the *peaceful fruit of righteousness (Heb. 12:11)*. We want dessert before we've eaten our vegetables, and a diet of nothing but sweets typically leads to an upset stomach. When observing the fruit of the Laodiceans, who consumed a steady diet of the desserts of wealth, comfort, and power, Jesus said He experienced the same symptoms.

Reaping Superficiality

Tina Griego, a columnist for the Denver Post, wrote the following review shortly after she had viewed the movie, *The Passion of the Christ*:

> It is a gauntlet thrown. A provocation…It demands we confront not just what we believe, but whether our lives offer testimony to those beliefs…It was a movie I very much wanted to see and very much didn't. Because I knew it would make me uncomfortable, because when it comes to matters of God and religion I am both unreconciled and full of longing. It is an ancient ache.[3]

This summarizes well where far too many in the modern church are with respect to following Jesus. Real depictions of the graphic and horrendous suffering of Christ on the Cross cause chaos within our souls, as would Communion if we would but properly observe it. I believe many in the church today feel that *ancient ache,* because when it comes to the issue of their religion they feel disconnected. They desire to know Jesus in a more real way—a way that effects their real lives. They see Jesus act a certain way, and hear His words that *command* them to. However, there is a disconnection between the example they see, and the lives they know they lead. In a word, their affliction is *superficiality.*

Superficiality is an inability to make a logical connection between what we believe, and what we observe to be true in our own lives. We all stumble in our attempts to follow Jesus, and if left unattended those temporary stumblings will eventually become sin patterns that bring about a feeling of disconnection from Him. Communion observed properly assaults superficiality, because it *demands* we confront not only our beliefs, but whether our lives support those beliefs. And that is a good thing, because we must face our temporary stumblings before they turn into destructive patterns. We must come under the searing light of God's convictions and the fellowship's confrontations, if we wish to honor the Table and discover where we remain un-reconciled with both.

God said that a mark of false teachers would be the proclamation of peace, when there was none. Communion is anything but the message of peace without chaos that we have made it today. No. *It is a gauntlet thrown, a provocation*—a wild and wooly, dangerous, and piercing look into the blackness of our souls. While it will eventually bring about the peaceful fruit of righteousness, to make it to that point demands initially that there is no peace.

> **Communion is anything but the message of "peace, peace," we have made it today. No! It is a gauntlet thrown, a provocation…**

If we deny the chaos, we then embrace a false peace that leads us into thinking wrong conduct is acceptable. This was precisely the disease of the Laodiceans: thinking they were rich and in need of nothing, when Jesus had a decidedly different assessment. When we make Communion the *excuser* of sinful patterns of living we have made it today, it transforms from ally to enemy. Instead of helping us to confront sin, deal with it, and be healed, it makes us superficial and shallow. It renders us unable to connect what we believe with how we live.

How Could we Have Gotten it so Wrong?

Would it be so wrong to infer that somehow the institutional church could have misinterpreted something so badly there seems to be such universal agreement on? How could it be that I stand against so many well-educated, well-intentioned ministers and raise a red flag over something as accepted as our current model of Communion? It is a question I have asked myself on numerous occasions. Is it that I am just theologically deluded, that I swim this far from the mainstream of conventional practice? I'm sure many current church leaders would say so. It has been widely accepted for many years now that Communion is to be held in large services, with a total focus on grace.

In the beginning of the book of Revelation, Jesus offers His seven churches both praise and warning. He even threatens to *remove their crowns* from before His throne if they fail to repent for their sins. Did they get it wrong? When Jesus came to earth, who did He constantly battle with? Did He enter the homes of sinners with a whip and fire in His eyes? Did He overturn tables of the merchants in the public square, as He did when He entered His Father's own house? It was the institutional church that had missed the point. It was the religious leaders, who had been given the benefit of studying the words of the prophets, who had gotten it all wrong. The religious establishment was what He ridiculed, and its teachers the only ones who endlessly challenged His authority, His person, and His message.

Throughout biblical history the story has been the same. God sent His Old Testament prophets to rebuke and correct His *own* people. He sent His last prophet, Jesus, to do the same thing. It has always been the religiously proud and set-in-their-ways—the ones who say, "We see" *(John 9:41)*, who have caused God to send His prophets into the world. God's anointed messengers always came proclaiming His tough truths to a church that had strayed, while typically preaching a message of hope to unbelievers. Who stoned the prophets? Who crucified Christ, the unbelievers? It was the leaders of organized religion, as it had always been, that were His constant nemesis. When they could not coerce or convince Him to join them in their error, they orchestrated His death. *Oh yes, the church can get it wrong.* The church has truly gotten this one wrong, and is now reaping the sure consequences.

> **Oh yes, the church can get it wrong. The church has truly gotten this one wrong.**

Ministering to All in the Body

Through many years of ministry, I have observed five basic types of people who call themselves believers. These types generally follow the pattern of the seeds of the Sower, along with one additional category. They are:

- The babes [first seed]: These are what we could call new believers in Christ. They are excited about their newfound faith, and many times much more open and bold about sharing it with others than the next two groups. However, they need to be mentored and discipled by those more mature, because they are extremely vulnerable to the deceptions and temptations of the evil one. Their roots haven't had time to develop, because they simply need sufficient time to come to abide in their Vine.

  For these, Communion presents a wonderful opportunity to observe and participate in the setting most conducive to witnessing how mature believers are to conduct themselves. They can join in this most real of all Christian ceremonies that will help lead them to maturity. It will take them beyond the basic principles of repentance from former works and faith in God *(Heb. 5:11-6:1)* and on to the meatier fare of learning discernment. This comes in the form of being able to discern one's own shortcomings before they go out to help others. As Jesus would put it: "Getting the log out of our own eye, so we can see clearly the speck in our brother's" *(Matt. 7)*.

- The perpetual babes [second seed]: These are those the writer of Hebrews spoke of, who just can't seem to bring themselves to a deeper and more mature faith. They simply refuse to *practice* what they learn. They have been to all the seminars and retreats, listened to all the tapes, perhaps even memorized a few verses, and read the Bible occasionally. But the good feelings they get from all of this never last.

  They can't seem to put feet on their faith, and make much of it work in the real world. They display the façade of the believer, but there is no fruit of the Spirit visibly present in their lives. It is all milk and no meat, and the fault for this lies squarely with an American church with little more than milk offered on the menu. Jesus asks these people the question, "Why do you call Me 'Lord, Lord,' and yet do not do what I say" *(Luke 6:46)*?

Communion for these can be the key that opens the door, because Communion participation *demands* action. It requires serious reflection upon our personal place with God. It also requires serious reflection upon our place in, and impact upon, His body as a whole. This group will find marvelous opportunities here to chew on the meat of the good deeds that God has prepared beforehand for them *(Phil. 2:10)*, and to understand the importance of practicing their beliefs: both in the church, and in the community that the church is to be a part of. If they will just accept their Communion responsibilities, they stand a much better chance of being transformed into meat-eaters.

✦ The Laodiceans [third seed]: These are the ones who think they are rich, and in need of nothing, when nothing could be further from the truth. They think claiming Jesus' name and achieving worldly success somehow pleases Him. They are neither hot nor cold when it comes to the things that matter to God, because it is truly the world's riches that excite them. To these, Jesus is barely more than another trinket on their well-stocked shelves of the possessions that keep them elevated and secure in their own eyes. The riches of the world have choked their faith, and blinded their eyes to where they've lost any sense of their own perilous position. Any sin in their lives is quickly rationalized, and then dissolved through imbibing in their latest social gathering or financial expenditure.

These first 3 groups partake of of modern Communion ceremonies that allow them to *cover up* dangerous and practiced sin patterns, rather than confronting them. Contrary to what they are taught by their religious leaders, they *eat and drink judgment upon themselves,* as they further the delusion. They become superficial people, both in the world and in the church. Failing to deal with sin, while thinking they walk in the faith, always leads to self-deception and shallowness.

But it need not be so! For all of these types, Communion can be the Laodicean-buster! Here they can be taught the dangers of hypocrisy and lukewarmth. Here they could be forced to come face-to-face with a holy God, and the confrontational aspect of loving fellowship. Here the safe and secure world of temporal well-being and immaturity couldn't comfort them, and they would have to face their demons, if we would but biblically administer it.

- Fruit-bearers [fourth seed]: These are those who have learned *and* practiced the balanced life of John 15. They have formed an abiding relationship with Jesus, and then go relentlessly out to bear fruit in the good deeds He has prepared for them. They have learned that it is only in living for others, letting the love of Jesus flow through them into those lives they touch that they come to understand what it means to be functional disciples. They leave an indelible mark on those they come to know—the mark of the Gospel of their living God. They think nothing of self, and pour their lives out on a regular and consistent basis for the evangelism of the lost, and the discipleship of the saved. However, Satan leaves his traps for them as well. They are still sinners.

    Communion for disciples is a blessed time of reflection, fine-tuning, and intimate fellowship with both God and man. It is also a wonderful opportunity to do what they always do—what they know they were born to do—minister to those less mature in the faith. There is no better time than Communion for them to come to understand and bear the burdens of their weaker brothers, thus fulfilling Jesus' law *(Gal. 6:2)* and their ministry.

- The apostates: These are the Judases: those Paul called *hidden reefs in our love feasts (Jude 12)*. These are the betrayers: those doubly-dead and lawless who once knew God, but have become so trapped in pride and self-deception that they now go out deceiving others with their false dreams and doctrines. There is no place for them at the Table of the Lord, due to their perpetual and unrepentant hardness of heart. They must be, as Judas was, *dismissed with haste* from the proceedings, because they will only pervert and cause dissention in any body they are allowed to coexist with.

There is no message here to them except, "Leave." It is the very purpose of the Table that we avoid falling into this category. Those who take advantage of its power to cleanse and heal will have a much easier time avoiding the apostates.

It may be just coincidence, then, that there are four basic ways God provided to bring about His healing change in our lives: 1) the conviction of His Holy Spirit *(John 16:8)*, 2) the dissemination of His word *(2 Tim 3:16-17)*, 3) prayer *(Ps. 32:3-6)*, and, 4) involvement in the fellowship of other believers *(Jas. 5:16)*. It is no coincidence, however, that each of these four elements is to be found in the Passover/Communion ceremony, because it's God's perfect maintenance check-up for His beloved children. We will likewise examine four areas in Scripture as we seek a truer understanding of this most holy of ceremonies:

- ✢ The Passover and Exodus of the Jews.
- ✢ The Gospel accounts of Christ's last supper with His disciples in Matthew 26, Mark 14, Luke 22, and John 13-17.
- ✢ The church of Acts 2, and,
- ✢ Paul's Communion instructions in 1st Corinthians 11

In the consistent message of these teachings, we will discover an event full of power and the conviction of the Holy Spirit. We will reawaken a ceremony that can take us back in time to the church of Pentecost, and the indelible mark of intimate fellowship it fostered in all who partook of its wonders. John testified, "Truly, truly, I say to you, 'we speak that which we know, and bear witness of that which we have seen'" *(John 3:11)*. I have come to *know*, both through experience and the abundant testimony I have personally witnessed over many years, the biblical model of Communion can transform any believer's walk through regular, effective exposing of destructive sin-patterns. True Communion keeps the temporary sins we all will struggle with from becoming the emotional minefields of persistent sinful living.

No Fear

Like any change in the status quo, there will be some initial discomfort and resistance. Even those willing to try may find it difficult to fully participate at first. Yet if we will just press on, a most challenging and wonderful adventure awaits us! It is one that we will come to know as anything but the tepid and lukewarm experience it has become for most today.

At the Lord's Table I have seen lives transformed, formerly shut mouths singing in overflowing praise, lost souls won for Christ, and hard, dry pottery changed into soft, moldable clay spinning gladly upon the Potter's wheel! I have personally witnessed the reawakening of many self-deceived, tortured souls, shallow relationships given new substance, and superficial Sunday gatherers transformed into disciples with depth of faith and purpose.

I've witnessed the spiritually weak strengthened, the spiritually sick healed, and the spiritually asleep rise from the dead that Christ might shine His light anew upon them *(Eph. 5:14)*. Communion is about grace, yes. But it is also and equally about the Holy Spirit bringing to our remembrance those un-reconciled roadblocks we have created between Himself and us through sincere self-examination and confession. It is all done within an environment of intimate fellowship. With that comes the power to act upon His convictions, and to put sinful practices behind us so that healing might begin.

Communion is the single-most healing proceeding anyone who will fully engage can involved in. It is God's supreme gift—the *spike*—given specifically for the emotional and spiritual well-being of His people. Communion is a masterfully devised event that moves us decisively towards dismantling the curse of superficiality currently yielding too many *complacent souls* in the church.

When put in Communion's environment, it is amazing to see how quickly formerly unreceptive people respond to the surgical work of the Holy Spirit. Believers and unbelievers alike are irresistibly attracted to the perfect balance of discipline and grace they all crave. People invite friends, because once understood and experienced the Table comes to be viewed with excitement and anticipation. Former participants I have not seen for years return from out of town and ask, "Are you still doing that Communion thing? When's the next one?" Is this the way the members of your church feel about the Lord's Supper? Is it the way you feel about it?

This work is a guide to what I believe God instituted to be our consistent and deeply revealing wake-up call—our recovery program from practiced sin-addictions that can lead to all manners of emotional dysfunction. It is a ceremony that God ordained to remind us of our continual need to examine ourselves, and face truthfully our standing before Him in light of the piercing truths of His Word. It is *a regular gauntlet thrown down*, to do something concrete about the wicked ways He will always reveal when we are obedient.

This wonderful opportunity—this ultimate weapon we have been given to fight the cursed sleep that has made our spiritual eyes heavy—this blessed reminder of the reality of the healing power of confession, prayer, humility, and repentance, isn't some new revelation. Rather, it is an ancient ceremony. But it has lost

> **This is not some new revelation. Rather, it is an ancient ceremony that has lost something in a church looking too much like the world.**

something in an American culture that seeks worldly comfort instead of spiritual truth, and a church that looks far too much like it. I close with this true story of a young man brought from hypocrisy and deception to the truth, via one biblically observed Communion ceremony.

Jeremy [all names used in stories are fictitious] sporadically attended our small group, graduated from high school, and I lost track of him until he suddenly reappeared in my life some fifteen years later. In the beginning, this young man lived a relatively worldly life. He was unwilling to commit himself fully to Christ, and far more committed to perfecting his rock-n-roll guitar skills than pursuing a relationship with God. One of the last things he did with us before leaving for college was to attend one of our Communion services.

When I next saw him those many years later, he was touring the country leading worship songs which he had written. He now used those considerable musical gifts to spread the Gospel, and had become a dedicated disciple of Jesus. I asked him about the miraculous turnaround in his life, and what it was that sparked the commitment I now saw. He said simply, "That Communion service I attended in your group before I left for college exposed me as the phony I was. It made me think." Here was a young man who had come from darkness to light, and from preaching a message of worldliness to one of life, hope, love, and encouragement! Here was a young man who had, and would continue to, change lives with the Gospel. It had all been made possible through one simple ceremony that has always been there for us—one ordained to expose the posers we all can become, *make us think*, and transform us into disciples.

So to answer the question, "Whatever happened to the Passover:" we've simply lost the ancient and intimate environment of it. We've lost the passion and reverence for that most important admonishment to examine ourselves as a *prerequisite* for partaking. It's been replaced by a *private, token, and not terribly upsetting look* at our un-reconciled issues. That has created an ancient ache, as God convicts us to get back to a Communion ceremony where the necessary chaos of self-examination precedes the peace of grace that can only follow the chaos.

Practicing the Lord's Table consistently, obediently, and biblically can bring emotional healing back into the church where it belongs, preserve our battle-readiness through good times and bad, and keep the sons and daughters of Adam and Eve bright-eyed and bushy-tailed for the often arduous journeys of the faith. So join me, if you will, in a hopefully eye-opening walk through the incredible riches God has awaiting in an intimate Passover/Communion experience. Understand why Jesus said of this ceremony alone, on the night His culminating victory over death was to unfold, "I have *earnestly desired* to eat this Passover with you." Embrace the love that waits for you there in abundance. But also fully embrace Christ's admonishments that wait for you there, and reap the boundless benefits from the healing power of *The Lost Supper*.

III. A LOVE TO EMBRACE, AN ADMONISHMENT TO CONSIDER

According to the opening verse of John 13 *(NIV)*, Jesus was on a mission at His Passover. That mission was to show His disciples the *full extent* of His love. What person ever received the full extent of Christ's love without knowing both the grace and persistent admonishments of the God-Man? The teachings and deeds Jesus displayed during the Passover were, indeed, a perfect representation of the *full extent* of His love. Hebrews 12 tells us it is *for* discipline that we endure, and that no loving father would fails to discipline his son. It also tells us that if we don't experience discipline, then we become *illegitimate* children and not sons. Jesus disciplines us for our good, that we might be able to share in His holiness and understand true love.

What better definition of Communion could we give than *an experience of sharing in His holiness*? If understanding the full extent of Christ's love—symbolically eating His body and drinking His blood—is not this, then what? How then could Jesus possibly show the full extent of His love to His flock while leaving out the disciplines of teaching, correcting, and training them in righteousness *(2 Tim. 3:16)*?

The full extent of God's love is displayed through the assurance of His grace, *along with* embracing sound teaching, discipline, and admonishment. The totality of Scripture, both Old and New Testaments, concerns God reassuring and encouraging us with His tender mercies, while teaching, admonishing, and correcting us to perfect us in His holiness. These blessings from God together are life to those He calls *friend*. Christ's teaching and deeds at the Passover with His disciples are the perfect picture of this. Together, they make the complete meal—and also draw the complete picture of the likeness of the Preparer of it—to see to our emotional and spiritual health.

The Lost Supper

In all Gospel accounts, the first act of Jesus at the Passover meal was to identify Judas Iscariot, when He said, "[The betrayer] is he who will dip his bread in the cup with me." In John 13:2, we witness this same event, signifying that at that point in time the Passover had begun. The ceremony concludes, again in all gospel accounts, with Jesus leading His disciples over the Brook Kidron to the Garden of Gethsemane, where the crucifixion passion play would begin. In John, this concluding event occurs at the beginning of chapter 18. Until I began to compare the account of John to the other Gospels, I had failed to see that all that transpired between John 13 and 18 occurred *at the Passover*. Here is by far the most complete account of Jesus' teaching and conduct at this event, and it beautifully paints a picture of the balance of love and admonition of which I speak.

> **All that transpired between John 13 and 18 occurred at the Passover.**

[Author's Note: There is a controversial verse at the end of John 14, where Jesus says, "Arise, let us be going." It is found nowhere in any of the other gospel accounts. Some theorize they got up at this point, and went to some other location between the upper room and the Brook Kidron. Some say they retired to another room in the house. Some say Jesus spoke metaphorically about putting into practice all He had taught them. Though the true meaning of this statement is not revealed to us, His remaining message to them in chapters 15 to 17 was very much a part of the Passover teaching of that final night. There is no indication that circumstances changed, or that the message had shifted to another scene, or focus. Whatever the reason, I believe Jesus decided to stay there in the upper room for the remainder of His message. There is no sign of movement from the group between this point and John 18. By failing to mention it, the other three Gospels would seem to agree with this assessment.]

Why is it so important to understand the account of the Passover in John? Consider: with the exception of the Sermon on the Mount, the most focused, powerful teaching of Jesus' entire ministry unfolded that very night. It included:

✦ His proclamation of being the way, the truth, and the life.

- ✦ The prophecy of His death, resurrection, and return to the throne.

- ✦ Foretelling of the work and character of the Holy Spirit coming to succeed Him.

- ✦ The Vine and branches: His restatement of the Great Commandment, and the picture of the balanced life of the disciple.

- ✦ Prophecies concerning coming persecutions for the disciples, and,

- ✦ Reassurances of the character and love of the Father for them.

In addition to Jesus' teaching, consider the impact of His deeds at the Passover:

- ✦ The washing of feet: Jesus' first act was to kneel down and cleanse the feet of the disciples, as He showed them one more time the Master was there to serve. He then told them to follow this example by serving one another. This was part of another message he wanted to leave for all who would come before His Table of Sacrifice for ages to come, namely…

- ✦ The cleansing of the fellowship: His next act was to confront Judas, this *devil in their midst*. Jesus released Judas to accomplish His evil deed without delay. How long He had labored with this traitor, even as He knew of Judas's eventual treachery. At last, Judas was dispatched to his destiny, to pay an eternal price. At last, Jesus could impart the most important teaching of His ministry on earth. For just as He had cleansed the Temple of its moneychangers, He had now cleansed His fellowship of the one in charge of their treasury—their *moneychanger*.

> **The first two acts of Jesus were done to ensure the cleansing of the fellowship.**

This means that the first two acts of Jesus at the Passover were *to ensure the cleansing of the fellowship*. I will spend a great deal of time later discussing how we have ignored our responsibilities to properly fence the Table, and thus opened ourselves to the proper judgment of God. Would that our administrators today note how careful Jesus was to guard His flock from impostors, and do likewise.

✦ Confronting sin: Jesus made it absolutely clear that Communion was to be a time of righteous confrontation. His earthly existence neared an end, and the curtain fell on superficiality of any kind. After dismissing Judas, He turned to Peter as he delivered his, "I'll defend you to the end" speech. Jesus glared at Peter, and told him that most certainly Peter would deny Him. When Phillip asked Jesus to show them the Father, he likewise became the target of Jesus' rebuke. He questioned Phillip's knowledge of His words, and his understanding of who He was.

These were just a few of His stinging admonishments suffered by the disciples. Jesus had a message to impart to them that all of life would hang upon. He had a prayer for them that all of life would come from. It was time to chew on every word He spoke, and consider every move He made. It was a time for reverent observance of the Man, and the ceremony.

✦ The high priestly prayer: The final act of Jesus among them was to seal His disciples through intercessory prayer. Through this act, He handed the keys to the kingdom of heaven on earth over to them. In this final display of incomprehensible love and grace, God entrusted His perfect plan into the hands of imperfect sinners. The charge was passed from the Father, to the Son, to the disciples in a prayer that would forever anoint them for their mission on earth.

Throughout John's Passover account, there is a noticeable pattern to Christ's teachings. It is a pattern that is critical to understanding the full extent of Christ's love available to us in the Passover/Communion experience. This pattern is found in His balanced teaching of love and grace, and warning and admonition. Jesus always taught this way. He could do no different, because it was who He was: the One who came to save the world, and the One who came to judge it.

Jesus was indeed full of grace and truth. He was full of a love that we always need to embrace when we think we are unloved or unforgiven. Yet, He was also full of truth and the admonishments we need to consider when we willfully stray into the lusts and deceptions of the flesh. He never let those who followed Him live in a state of self-deception. He would attack instantly any hint of superficiality in anyone He came into contact with. Jesus never spared the rod as He advanced the cause of truth, any more than he would spare grace as He advanced the cause of love.

> **Jesus never spared the rod when it came to advancing the cause of truth, any more than he would spare grace when it came to advancing the cause of love.**

We see this balance of truth and grace in the keys the early churches displayed *(Acts 9)*. They enjoyed peace, were built up, and moved forward in the fear of the Lord *and* the comfort of the Holy Spirit. Embracing this balance caused the church to *increase*. Solomon tells us by mercy and truth iniquity is atoned for, *and* by the fear of the Lord we are able to keep from evil *(Prov. 16:6)*. Through grace *and* truth iniquity is atoned for. Through the fear of the Lord *and* the comfort of the Holy Spirit the church is kept from evil, increases in numbers, and enjoys peace.

In Matthew 26 and Mark 14, we find Jesus and the disciples singing a hymn during His Passover. Psalms 113-118 are known as the "Passover Hymns," because they were commonly sung during the ceremony. These are believed by most scholars to be the hymns sung at the Passover referred to by Matthew and Mark. In these as well, we find this balance of love and admonishment. They are filled with songs of praise for God's ability to bless His people, and deliver them from sin and death. At the same time, they speak of the idols men make that bring them down, the importance of fearing Him, the depths sin can take us to, the importance of keeping our commitments to God in the sight of the church, and the severe discipline of our God that convicts deeply, yet never abandons us. These Psalms are the perfect picture of the highs and lows that are the stuff Communion is made of to this day.

The prophet Hosea encourages us to return to the God who tears us down to heal us, and who wounds us to bandage us—promising that

God will always revive us so that we may live before Him *(Hos. 6:1-2)*. Tearing to heal, wounding to bandage, breaking down to revive, and striking to raise up that we may live before Him is ever and always God's way. It is the way of Communion as well. Together, these two qualities of love and admonishment are the key to sharing in Christ's holiness, experiencing the full extent of His love, and also the keys to a fruitful Communion service.

The Two Critical Questions

Two questions should be posed every time we come to the Lord's Table: 1) is there a love that needs to be embraced, and, 2) is there an admonishment that needs to be considered? As to the first question Jesus says, "And you have perseverance, and have endured for My name's sake. You have not grown weary. But I have this against you: that you have left your first love" *(Rev. 2:4)*. The church at Ephesus had gotten the admonishment and discipline down, but had evidently turned it in to a form of legalism. They had forgotten to embrace the love of Jesus, which eventually leads to hard-heartedness in some form or another.

Addressing the second question Paul says, "We proclaim Him, admonishing every man and teaching every man with all wisdom, so that we may present every man complete in Christ" *(Gal. 1)*. So much of scripture is admonishing in nature, but we cannot live by admonishment alone, any more than we could live by grace alone, or we would lose heart and grow wearied in our pursuit of Christ. A balance of both is what is needed, and a balance of both is what Jesus both lived and taught at His Passover.

When we examine all of the verses in the New Testament that deal with the Passover/Communion *(approximately 241 in all: Matt 5 and 26, Mark 14, Luke 22, John 13-17, Acts 2 and 1 Cor. 11)*, we find that approximately 54 of them are neutral commentary, 59 of them espouse God's grace and love, 103 are instructional, and 25 are admonishing in nature. Would Abraham have been found worthy to have received the covenant if not for his trial with Isaac? Would Moses have been found worthy to lead the Exodus, or receive the Ten Commandments, without enduring his forty years in the desert? Would David have been found to be *a man after God's own heart, willing to do all His will*, without enduring his trials with Saul?

Jesus said that Paul would be shown just how much he would have to suffer for His name's sake *(Acts 9:16)*, and then brought His words to pass. Just prior to Peter—the rock upon which Jesus would build His church—denying Him, Jesus told him that Satan had demanded permission to sift him like wheat. He didn't keep that sifting from happening, but He said He would pray for Peter's faith to prevail in the end. Jesus also knew Peter would get the ship righted again, and that when he did he would fulfill his destiny as that rock, and go forth strengthening his brothers *(Luke 22)*. Would Peter have been found worthy to lead Christ's church on earth had he not first suffered the striking rebuke of his own denials?

Our greatest example of God striking to heal is Jesus Himself, who was *pierced* for our sin, and *crushed* for our iniquity. Isaiah tells us that the *chastening* for our redemption would fall upon Him, and by His *injury* we would be healed *(Isa. 53:5)*. Could there be any greater example of the most severe striking in history ever inflicted, and all to bring about the greatest healing ever accomplished? The teaching and life-example Jesus displayed throughout His incarnation was consistently, and without fail, a blend of admonishment and grace. True to form, in John's account of the Passover we find:

- John 13:4-17: Washing of the disciples' feet [a love to embrace]
- Verse 10: Judas singled out as one with hard heart [an admonishment to consider]
- Verse 18-30: Judas dismissed [an admonishment to consider]
- Verse 31-37: Peter rebuked for boasting [an admonishment to consider]
- John 14:1-7: Jesus comforting the disciples [a love to embrace]
- Verse 8-11: Philip's rebuke for his lack of faith [an admonishment to consider]
- Verse 15-31: Jesus promising the Holy Spirit [a love to embrace]
- John 15:1-17: The teaching of the vine and branches—the balanced life of the disciple [mixture of a love to embrace and an admonishment to consider]
- Verse 18-27 and John 16:1-4: The warning of persecutions to

come [an admonishment to consider]
- ✦ Verse 5-29: Promises of the resurrection [a love to embrace]
- ✦ John 17: The high priestly prayer [a love to embrace].

We all lose our first love at times, refuse to forgive or believe we are forgiven ourselves, and become guilt-ridden. We all, likewise, refuse instruction and discipline at times, becoming unrepentant and hypocritical. The demeanor of Jesus at the Passover reveals the same mixture of grace and admonishment we see in Paul's Communion instruction in 1st Corinthians. They are completely consistent. When we remove either the love or the admonishments, we end up with something far less meaningful and far less transforming than the original plan intended.

Jesus wanted them to understand, in this final message, both the love He had for them and the daunting task ahead of them. He knew they would need to learn to accept correction if they were to know joy in the midst of pruning and trials. An understanding of discipline would bring endurance in the midst of them, so they could be made *perfect and complete, lacking in nothing (Jas.1:2-4)*. He also knew their own sinful natures, the temptations facing them in the world, and the hardships and persecutions they would confront from it all would require they understand His abiding love and grace, there in abundance to pick them up when they stumbled.

If we think God is all about striking, we become Pharisees in servitude to a cruel taskmaster. If we think God is all about healing, we become what the Bible calls *illegitimate children*: hypocrites whose deeds prove they don't understand the fear of God. It is through engaging *both* His

> **We cannot remove the striking from the healing. Otherwise, we are left with a counterfeit healing.**

love to embrace, and His admonishments to consider, that we truly come to understand that *full extent* of God's love. Admonishment is an integral part of the Communion teaching, for if we remove the striking from healing we are left with a counterfeit healing, and Prodigal Sons called home before they have learned the important lessons found only in eating pods with pigs.

I close this chapter with God speaking to those administrators of His altar who were not properly admonishing His people. His warnings are very applicable to what we see happening in the Christian church today:

> You are presenting defiled food upon My altar. But you say, "How have we defiled Thee?" in that you say, "The Table of the Lord is to be despised." But when you present the blind for sacrifice, is it not evil? And when you present the lame and sick, is it not evil *(Mal. 1: 7-8)*?

God rejected lame and sick sacrifices on His altar then, and He still does today. Paul told the Corinthians that the consequence of such sacrifices in their observances caused *sickness*. Presenting unworthy sacrifices bred sickness then, and it does now. It was evil in God's sight then, and it's evil now.

> But now, will you not entreat God's favor that He may be gracious to you? With such an offering on your part, will He receive any of you kindly?" says the Lord of Hosts. "Oh, that there were one among you who would shut the gates that you might not uselessly kindle fire on My altar! I am not pleased with you," says the Lord of Hosts, "nor will I accept an offering from you" *(vs. 9-10)*.

God has given us the perfect instrument to clean the table of His new tabernacle—the one that dwells in our hearts and minds *(1 Cor. 6:19)*—but He asks a piercing question of those who would administer it: "Is there anyone among you that will have the courage and conviction of My Word to shut the gates against those who would defile My Table by coming with impure, unrepentant hearts?" He searches for courageous shepherds who will confront the Cancer of un-reconciled, un-confessed sin now infecting and debilitating the church, that we might seek His favor, and that the grace so available to us at Communion might be *real*.

When administrators of the Table, who should know better, allow those they know are entangled in all forms of habitual sin patterns they have no interest in dealing with to come before Him in their *lame* condition, it is sin in God's sight. He refuses to accept such sacrifices.

> And now this commandment is for you, O priests. "If you do not listen and if you do not take it to heart to give honor to My name," says the Lord of hosts. "Then I will send the curse upon you, and I will curse your blessings. Indeed, I have cursed them already, because you are not taking it to heart" *(Mal. 2:1-2)*.

Can we honestly look at the condition of the church in America, and fail to see the severity of the *curses* God is employing to try to get our attention? How do we fail to see His judgments manifested in our ranks, as we come to resemble more every day people who do not believe at all? The curses of superficiality and shallowness run rampant in the Christian church in America. The polls all show it. A world increasingly disinterested in what the church has to say mocks it. The faithful become increasingly numb to it, and daily become more disconnected from their Christian lives. If God were blessing as we suppose, and not cursing, this wouldn't be so. Malachi concludes:

> But as for you, you have turned aside from the way. You have caused many to stumble by [your] teaching...You are not keeping My ways, but are showing partiality in the instruction *(vs. 8-9)*.

When we make the Altar all about grace, and neglect to include the admonishments that are equally a part of it, we do indeed *show partiality* in the instruction. When our administrators do that, they do indeed *turn aside* in sin and take their sheep with them.

> **When we allow those mired in continual, unrepentant sin to come time and time again before the Table of the Lord in meaningless repetition, we *do* defile it.**

When we allow those mired in continual, unrepentant sin to come time and time again before the Table of the Lord in meaningless repetition, we *do* defile it. We uselessly kindle fire on His altar, and His anger burns against both unrepentant sinners, and those who allow their transgression to go on unopposed.

God cries out for obedient, more mature administrators to lovingly correct the less mature. Nowhere is this needed more than at the Table of grace and judgment. More often than not, it is another human being God uses to bring His hard words of admonishment into our lives, so that the leaven of habitual sin patterns can be removed. We can then become a new lump of dough that He can once again mold, as we are revitalized in our personal walks through *unleavened* sincerity and truth.

As we approach the Table of the Lord, let us reverently consider the mood, the attitude, the spirit, and the awesome power of the moment. Let us realize that no other venue but Communion could have been selected to contain it, and meditate on the totality of Christ's actions and message at His Passover. Let us place ourselves in the story masterfully painted in John's account so reverent fires of awe can burn anew for our God, and His most holy of ceremonies! Jesus still confronts us there with an admonishment we need to consider. Jesus still forgives us there with a boundless love we need to embrace. There, He still intercedes in High Priestly prayers for us. At the Communion Table Jesus still prepares us for the daunting task of trying to live with integrity in a fallen world.

IV. MINISTERING AND EXPERIENCING ADMONISHMENT

> Nothing can be more cruel than the tenderness that consigns another to his sin. Nothing can be more compassionate than the severe rebuke that calls a brother back from the path of sin. 4

I once attended an Episcopal Easter Sunday service in the desert of California, where my wife and I often enjoyed our spring vacation. I remember being struck by the absolute beauty of this place: towering vaulted ash-paneled ceilings, glass everywhere looking out to crystal blue desert skies, palm trees, and ornate flower gardens. The building was as inviting a place as one could imagine, and all on a typically gorgeous spring morning in the desert. There was narry a cloud in the sky, a diverse symphony of birds were singing, and the ever-present smell of orange blossoms filled the air. I praised God for providing such a setting for worship.

But shortly after we were seated, I noticed two men who walked down the aisle and sat in the front row. There were hundreds in attendance that morning, but these two stood out because they wore matching bright white-and-black cowboy shirts and blue jeans: attire that was hardly the order of the day among mostly affluent retired folks. A man next to me noticed my interest in them, and said, "Those two are a couple of real characters. They ride up every Sunday on their loud motorcycles, and always sit in that same spot in the front row. They're very devoted to the church…and they're gay."

Dark clouds began gathering over my beautiful spring morning, as my mind painted an inevitable portrait of what was surely coming that made me want to get up and leave. Not long after the ceremony began, my fears were confirmed. Communion was served, Paul's instructions ended with "Do this in remembrance of Me," no warnings at all were given, and everyone in a church of several hundred [save me and one other couple] got up and went forward. And yes, the two gay motorcycle jockeys were the first to joyously partake from the very hands of the smiling priest.

My spirit recoiled! I was at once saddened and sickened at the sight of such a desecration of the holy Sacraments—the very ceremony God gave to confront such lawlessness used rather to enforce it. I suddenly knew how Jesus felt when the superficiality and self-delusion of the Laodiceans caused Him to throw up. But, the truth be told, this is more the practice than the exception in the modern church. We promote a costless grace, and thereby desecrate a Table that cost our Passover Lamb everything. It is a grace without repentance, and mercy assumed without conviction of sin.

> We promote a costless grace that desecrates a Table that cost our Passover Lamb everything.

Homosexuality is the same as any other sin-addiction, mind you. But it is a very good example of the type of sin that one *practices,* and that leavens every part of life. Like any other sin, it can be repented of. Like any other sin, it needs to be confronted by the church. We are reaping the consequences of allowing only the Lord's *tenderness* a place at the Communion Table. Through ignoring the Lord's admonishments, cover-ups are allowed to survive, thereby consigning those participating unworthily to their sin. The *severe rebuke* of both God and a brother or sister in Christ comes through the self-examination process, and its *compassionate* goal is to call us back from sin. That is why Bonhoeffer affirms that admonishment can be one of the most compassionate things we can do for a friend trapped in destructive sin patterns.

A Necessary Pressure

> The first step is always to admit where we are so we can leave where we are. Take whatever desire of the flesh we have, lay it on the table, admit it, and stop making

provision for it. "All things" have been given to [Jesus]," and He has set us free from "All things." The problem is that we do not want to be free from our Little Precious that feeds the flesh and, hence, gives the enemy the right to attack and oppress. 5

Where repentance is concerned, the road to life with Christ for the seasoned disciple is the same as it is for the sinner newly embracing salvation's call. Jesus, the mediator of grace and the Lamb of sacrifice, still stands before the sinner—saved or not—proclaiming, "Repent, for the kingdom of heaven is at hand." For saint or sinner, the bridge of grace between heaven and hell is founded upon the cornerstone of repentance. Grace wasn't intended to be suspended above it, detached and free, carrying the weight of our sin alone.

Without taking whatever desire of the flesh we have, laying it on the table, admitting it, and no longer granting it free access to control us, true freedom from bondage is but a myth. No bridge will exist, apart from the vain illusions that it does—and that borne upon men's wishful dreams rather than God's righteous truth. Those who think they can conform God to their sin, and that their transgression can be divinely covered by grace apart from repentance in both deed and truth have bought into the modern church version of grace. That is what's killing us.

Over years of dumbing down the Gospel message, we have belittled repentance and magnified grace to where neither holds its original meaning or power. Neither is able to save. We think we can remain unrepentant, as we indulge our *Little Precious's that feed our flesh*, and yet walk with Jesus and be forgiven. Repentance has become insincere repetition in our evangelism, request without demand in our preaching, and a faint memory in our holy Communions.

> **Repentance has become insincere repetition in our evangelism, request without demand in our preaching, and a faint memory in our holy Communions.**

Without sincere and humble response to God's conviction in our heart-of-hearts, grace on the lips or in the mind becomes a part of the problem, rather than the solution.

Perhaps our best example of church discipline is found in Matthew 18, where biblical procedures for administrating it are established. If the offender is unrepentant, it proceeds from: 1) correcting him privately, to, 2) taking 2 or 3 others with you to correct him more firmly, to, 3) going to the leadership of the church with your concerns. If even that doesn't work, the church is to remove him from the fellowship—period. Tough medicine, yes—but mild compared to the hell on earth you will doom him to if you leave him alone in a state of self-delusion. This concept can and should be applied to the Communion setting, for intimate believers joined at the Table is a microcosm of "the church." Jesus did this very thing at the Passover by dismissing Judas [letting him be as an unbeliever], and justly admonishing the others.

Notice that it is in the small-group setting the Matthew 18 admonishment occurs, before it becomes an issue for the church. In Communion, under Paul's direct order to examine ourselves, we can enter into the Matthew 18 confrontational process one-to-one [reproving in private], or in small groups [by the mouths of two or three witnesses]. If a participant refuses admonition, they need to be as a tax gatherer at the Lord's Table and solemnly warned against participation in the Elements until they repent—end of story. Jesus refused to negotiate with Judas, as He did with anyone else who wanted to hold on to their idols while feigning allegiance to Him. His answer to them was always, and consistently, "This you lack. Go and..." It is so today to any and all who come to His Altar unrepentant, and unwilling to undergo the required self-examination.

In his contemporary-language version of the New Testament, *The Message*, Eugene H. Peterson records Paul's consistency with the Corinthians, as the church turns its back to sin in the body:

> I'm telling you that this is wrong. You must not simply look the other way and hope it goes away on its own. Bring it out in the open and deal with it in the authority of Jesus our Master. Assemble the community. I'll be present with you and our Master Jesus will be present in power. Hold this man's conduct up to public scrutiny.

> Let him defend it if he can! But if he can't, then out with him! It will be totally devastating to him, of course, and embarrassing to you. But better devastation and embarrassment than damnation. You want him on his feet and forgiven before the Master on the day of judgment *(1ˢᵗ Cor. 5)*. 6

If people mired in practiced, unrepentant sin refuse to deal with it we must warm them to abstain. As Paul would say, "Out with them!" This does not need to mean barring a participant from Communion forever, any more than it does in Matthew's discussion of church discipline. Under God's grace, there is always room for repentance and the re-establishment of fellowship. Such extreme measures are necessary sometimes, as they were with Judas, or there would have been no need for Matthew to say so. When the time comes to partake of the Elements, you want your brother or sister on their feet and forgiven if you truly love them. You need to be willing to speak truth to them to see to it that happens.

Oswald Chambers, in one of Christendom's most enduring devotionals, *My Utmost for His Highest,* follows both Boenhoeffer's and Paul's admonitions to those more mature in the fellowship:

> If a person cannot go to God, it is because he has something secret which he does not intend to give up. He may admit his sin, but would no more give up that thing than he could fly under his own power. It is impossible to deal sympathetically with people like that. We must reach down deep in their lives to the root of the problem, which will cause hostility and resentment toward the message. People want the blessing of God, but they can't stand something that pierces right through to the heart of the matter. If you are sensitive to God's way, your message as His servant will be merciless and insistent, cutting to the very root. Otherwise, there will be no healing. We must drive the message home so forcefully that a person cannot possibly hide, but must apply its truth.7

Michael Wells heads an unpretentious ministry called Abiding Life Ministries International. He is as close to a modern-day Paul as anyone you will ever know. He travels the hell-holes and backwaters of third world countries much of the year helping plant churches, training pastors and, in his words, "Bringing the people Jesus." God has given this man such simple yet profound wisdom. Michael has this to say about the concept of the holy pressure a proper self-examination is to engender, and its critical effect upon our lives from his newsletter, *Life Lines*:

> Coal is made up of somewhat random carbon molecules which under pressure get to a point where the best way they can fit is to be perfectly aligned. This causes the clarity of a diamond, which comprises perfectly arranged carbon. Something pitch black becomes crystal clear under pressure. Pressure is not a curse but a refining, and it lines my being up with God's will. 8

Such pressure is absolutely necessary for a fruitful Communion experience. Indeed, to bring about such holy pressure is, I believe, the admonishment to consider *itself*. People are dying these days for discipline in their spiritual walks. They'll deny they need it, fight it, and try to avoid it in any way possible. However, once pinned down and lovingly given no other path, the fruit always comes forth and they love it. Discipline is a critical element in the growth of any follower of Jesus and, while

> **People are dying these days for discipline in their spiritual walks.**

we all resist it initially, those who have been trained by it always glean the peaceful fruit of righteousness *(Heb. 12:11)*. Accepting this holy pressure is a necessity for the saint, whether it is from God's conviction, or His words spoken through the mouth of a brother.

The goal of any growth process in the Christian faith is a changed heart. God miraculously changes hearts during the conversion process. However, such cases are rare without bringing the fellowship of others into the equation when it comes to the sanctification process of a believer once converted. It is rarer still in the case of those whose hearts have become hardened over weeks, months, or perhaps years of superficial living in un-confessed sin. They may have been taught discipline. They may have even understood its function. Yet, until they have yielded to the process it will never bear fruit.

A Wonderful Place for a Nasty Business

John and Jesus came proclaiming it as the only door to salvation. Still today this process of the work of repentance is a nasty business. It *requires* of us an openness and vulnerability we are predisposed to shy away from. Whether from heaven [in the form of the Spirit's conviction], or earth [in the form of a brother's correction], it *demands* some discomforting pressure applied to our souls. Jesus admonished those He loved in the hopes that the fruits of repentance would be borne.

The work of repentance takes two parties working in harmony in the fellowship: 1) one more mature in a given area of life willing to minister admonishment, and, 2) another who is willing to receive it in the area in which they stumble. The success of the Passover/Communion revolves around those who are willing to give, and experience, the admonishment critical to a real self-examination. It demands allowing the Holy Spirit, working through the fellowship, to do His work of convicting us and drawing us back to God.

Brothers and sisters in Christ involving themselves in loving admonition is how dealing with sin—and in the process finding emotional healing—gets done. It is also how it gets done in the Communion setting. Dietrich Bonhoeffer wrote this concerning the importance of conviction within fellowship in His book appropriately entitled, *Life Together*. It is an appropriate title because holy life together, under God's grace and instruction in the fellowship of the saints, is what Communion is all about:

> But God has put this Word into the mouth of men in order that it may be communicated to other men. When one person is struck by the Word, he speaks it to others. God has willed that we should seek and find His living Word in the witness of a brother—in the mouth of man…The Christ in his own heart is weaker than

the Christ in the word of his brother. His own heart is uncertain, his brother's is sure. 9

Christ confronted His disciples through both His deeds and words at the Passover. Among His first words there were, "Assuredly, I say to you, one of you will betray Me," revealing His willingness to confront whatever necessary to insure the purity of the night. His first deed there was to dismiss Judas the betrayer. Jesus came out swinging in a way He never had before with His own friends! He broke from the gate confronting sin and dismissing posers. Jesus put His disciples on notice that this would be a night where the One *most* mature would be administering admonishment. Those who heard would either be ready to accept it, or be shown the same door that had just closed on the behind of Judas.

Many times a person will have to listen to a brother or sister whom Christ has put in their lives who will speak loudly, because they refused to listen to His whispers. No tame table here—Miss Manners was not invited to this banquet! The reason for the ineffectiveness of our modern observances cannot be placed at the feet of God. Jesus displayed that night the same willingness to confront and deal with sin He is willing to display today. It isn't for lack of His plan, but for the fact the church passed on that plan.

As I examined the process of the 12-step, I discovered that Communion, done properly, was *that plan*. Given these programs found their genesis in Christianity anyway, I have often wondered why the founders didn't just call it what it was. For whatever reason, the fact remains that the 12-step *is* a form of Communion, and uncomfortable confrontation and admonition is very much a part of their plan. I will periodically refer to the 12-step program, and their genesis in the Communion ceremony to prove this point.

> **Communion, properly done, was the model for the 12-step!**

There is a reason that these programs employ as a foundational principle the concept of *sponsorship*, where recovering addicts team up with each new member of the group to help them through the process. It is because one brother needs another who will confront him, and speak God's truth to him. There are many times one person is stronger in an area than another. Jesus sent His disciples out two-by-two, because He knew they would face many trials and temptations as they went out into the world. There would be times when they would need to encourage one another, and also times when they would need to admonish one another. It is no different with Communion, or any other endeavor of fellowship for that matter. The wisest man who ever lived said, "Woe to the one who falls when there is not another to lift him up" *(Eccl. 4:10).*

It is the church's refusal to require the same process from their addicts that has caused Communion to become the impotent ritual it is today. It will be absolutely necessary that courageous shepherds [both pastors and small group leaders], worthy of their trust and true to their ministry, take a page from these programs and lead us back from the malaise. If they fail, we will continue to waste this God-given golden opportunity to face the pressure that can and will turn a lump of black coal into the light of the world, crystal in its clarity and shining with diamond-like purpose. This is where God gave His children a wonderful place to enter into the nasty business of admonishment.

Dr. Larry Crabb says this about a very real connection that takes place between believers when they both administer and experience proper doses of admonishment, discipline, and love in their fellowships:

> If the connection consists of profound acceptance, looking for the good, and the ability to see bad without retreating, then friendship exists in a relationship that can bear the weight of advice, rebuke and failure, and richly enjoy the pleasures of encouragement…If, however, the connection goes beyond acceptance to include penetrating wisdom and spiritual discernment, then friendship has deepened into shepherding. 10

It is through this ingeniously devised tool of Communion that the process of discipline can be initiated in a loving environment, but it must involve the confrontational element of admonishment between two people walking the road of confession together. Discipline and confrontation go hand-in-hand, and through it friendship deepens into shepherding. Jesus didn't try to shepherd without confrontation, particularly through the example He set for us at the Passover meal, so why try?

Paul also said to the Corinthians [his favorite targets for confrontation, it would seem], "For though I caused you sorrow by my letter, I do not regret it, though I did regret it… for I see that that letter caused you sorrow, though only for a while…I now rejoice, not that you were made sorrowful, but that you were made sorrowful to the point of repentance. For you were made sorrowful according to the will of God, in order that you might not suffer loss in anything through us. For the sorrow that is according to the will of God produces repentance without regret, leading to salvation, but the sorrow of the world produces death. For behold what earnestness this very thing, this godly sorrow, has produced in you: what vindication of yourselves, what indignation, what fear, what longing, what zeal, what avenging of wrong" *(2 Cor. 7:11)*.

God's conviction coming to men through confrontation is vividly portrayed here. Paul was unafraid to mete out stern warnings, along with his graceful encouragements, because he had personally witnessed the evidence of the fruit of the Spirit taking root in the Corinthians as a direct result of his refusal to compromise either.

When we are caught in the webs of Satan's deceptions, the *last* thing we need is for someone to tell us we're doing fine. What we need is true prophets who care more about our spiritual maturity than their popularity, or keeping enough warm bodies in the seats of their churches to pay the overhead. We need brothers and sisters who will come boldly into our lives, helping us to expose and deal with the iniquities that have blinded our eyes.

> **When we are caught in the webs of Satan's deceptions, the *last* thing we need is for someone to tell us we're doing fine.**

The Perfect Setting for the Difficult Task

Anyone who has tried to be a prophet of admonition in the life of another has known the anxieties that emerge when wondering when and how to begin cutting through the cloak of self-deception without offending. It is even more frightening for the victim of that deception, who feels God's hand heavy upon him, to try to face it. In addition to the difficulties involved in administering or receiving the ministry of admonishment, trying to find the right time and place to do it complicates matters even more.

Do we approach a brother to correct him privately [per Matthew 18 discipline] during a Sunday service? Do we approach him at a small group function? A party? Do we just call him on the phone and say, "There's something I've been meaning to discuss with you?" Perhaps. Yet, if we begin to take seriously Paul's admonition to *examine ourselves* within the Communion setting—and follow Jesus' model of resolve and willingness at His Passover—we will find that God gave us this ceremony as the ideal environment to grant both parties those golden moments for confrontation! It is the perfect place for submission to the hard words He may bring through our brother who loves us, and is concerned and courageous enough to speak.

Why is it that people find it so easy to confess to their therapists, or at their AA meetings? Why do people find it so much easier to confront others, or their own demons, in those settings? It's because they are going in to an environment where confession and confrontation is expected! One alcoholic may not confront another one on the street, but they will at the AA meeting. One brother probably wouldn't confront another in church, or at lunch, but they will during an event the Lord has prepared for just such things. This is *the* anointed and ordained environment God has given His children for personal confrontation, and administration of the process of discipline in the church.

The small group Communion environment is the setting God provided for His children to establish the intimacy necessary for administering and accepting admonishment. It is therefore incumbent upon those more mature to do the uncomfortable, yet imminently rewarding, job of seeing to it that process is carried out. Small groups were never intended to take on the form of mini-church services, where people are preached to instead of personally confronted and challenged. Again: a nasty business this work of admonishment, but mild when compared to falling into the hands of a sometimes angry God who watches carefully over His Table of sacrifice. Admonishment is also preferable by far, to living in the clutches of the superficiality that is always brought on by living a lie.

When we are gathered in a setting where the *commandment* of the moment is to examine ourselves, where discipline is expected and encouraged, and where the small-group environment has already been established that reassures the self-deceived of a safe place to dump, this process does not have to be awkward at all. What better place or time than where the goal is self-examination? What better setting than among a group of people involved in trusting relationships?

It was the trust that Christ's disciples had learned to put in Him and each other over time that carried them through their own confrontations. Small groups gathered around the Lord's Table provide *the* place—God's place—to effectively administer and experience admonishment, because people can take advantage of those pre-existent friendships the small group alone affords. Once proper teaching and courageous example has established that environment, participants come to know that they can take advantage of the opportunity to confess, just like they would at an AA meeting or in the therapist's office.

Not Forgetting the Grace

I know these past chapters have been hard to digest, and at this point your soul may be feeling rather heavy. However, breaking curses long embedded, through denial and rationalization, take some shock treatment to begin to address. But let us never forget that Communion also provides the perfect setting to engage with great love and care. You always take a chance on wounding the spirit of another when you enter in to this process. People used to living superficial lives have often erected elaborate defensive schemes to keep the truth from getting through. Breaking through these schemes can bring to the surface a vast array of emotions, pain, and even physical manifestations. This is where the tender mercies of God's sacrifice we also remember at the Lord's Table will comfort us This is where He will run to the gate to welcome His returning prodigals who have had the courage to honor His Table!

As we enter in to Communion confrontation, we must constantly keep in mind discipline can become legalistic and Pharisiacal if not done with patient, enduring love—the kind of love represented in the Elements. Properly understood, administered, and monitored, discipline can be accomplished effectively in and through God's love here at the table of grace. Jesus was openly confrontational at His Passover, and yet didn't alienate His disciples, because they had come to trust in His love.

Like Christ's disciples, Communion participants need to know through immersion in enduring and faithful relationships, there is an element of love and caring established among already intimate brothers and sisters. This will be, for both shepherd and flock, a night that will push the faith envelope of anyone who seriously participates to the limit. It will be a time where all will be challenged by the Holy Spirit. It will be a time when all gathered will be taking an enduring, honest look at the sinfully natured, truly ugly beast that prowls within. Communion will be that event where people can break through, as they take steps toward maturity and sanctification.

Here at the Lord's Table the individual and the body come together to at once appreciate God's unfathomable gift of grace, and enter in to the holy pressure of His pruning process. When Jesus is allowed into any group—really allowed and invited to convict and purge sin—the pressure comes. Whenever the truth is preached, and the processes set forth in His word experienced, the pressure comes! Chambers says of this:

> In the teachings of Jesus Christ the element of judgment is always brought out. It is the sign of the love of God. Never sympathize with someone who finds it difficult to get to God. God is not to blame. It is not for us to figure out the reason for the difficulty, but only to present the truth of God so that the Spirit of God will reveal what is wrong. *The greatest test of the quality of our preaching is whether or not it brings everyone to judgment.* When the truth is preached, the Spirit of God brings each person face to face with God Himself.

…and…

> The saint who satisfies the heart of Jesus will make other saints strong and mature for God. But the people used to strengthen us are never those who sympathize with

us. *In fact, we are hindered by those who give us their sympathy.* [emphasis mine] 11

Jesus has called us all to preach the truth to one another, and He never calls us to something He fails to enable us to do. There is no other setting more conducive to loving confrontation like Communion. The trust, closeness, integrity, and sense of loving community pre-established in the small-group fellowship sets the stage of confrontation-with-love. Lean on the Perfect Love. Lean on Jesus, and follow His Passover example of teaching a healthy balance of a love to embrace and admonishments to consider.

Preach truth. Refuse to grant sympathy to people looking for it as a way to continue the cover-ups. Honor the process of discipline. Minister and experience admonition: one soul to another. Participate in confrontational love, and enjoy the fruit. Jesus is glorified when His people confront one another in love, as they search for the reality of following Him, and learn to deal with their sinful natures.

> **God is glorified when His people confront one another in love, in their search for the reality of following His Son...**

When two or three gathered in His name present the truth of God, so that the Spirit of God will reveal what is wrong, He will be there. This will lead ultimately to the peaceful fruit of righteousness coursing through the veins of everyone courageous enough to administer and experience admonishment.

V. PRODIGALS, FATHERS, AND BROTHERS

The story the Prodigal Son offers us is a dramatic representation of one of Communion's primary functions: bringing prodigals home from a life of wandering. It reveals the heart of the Father for all His prodigals, and attitudes those more mature need to embrace as He does His work. According to Luke's account of this story:

> A certain man had two sons, and the younger of them said to his father, "Father, give me the share of the estate that falls to me." And he divided his wealth between them *(Luke 15:11-13)*.

Both the prodigal and the older brother were *sons*. The prodigal was nothing less than a full-blown blood relative and heir, just like the older brother. But the younger decided to squander his inheritance in favor of a life of rebellion, while the older decided to live in obedience—to *follow* in his father's footsteps. Christian men sons of their Heavenly Father and heirs of His kingdom, yet they are also sons of Adam, and heirs of his fallen-ness.

As sons of our Father we listen to what He has to say to us through His Word, prayer, and the testimony of others. We also try to follow Him by spreading His Gospel thorough our words and deeds. As sons of Adam, though, we are also apathetic, abandoning, rebellious, and stubborn. In our prodigal moments, we oftentimes tell God we want to go squander our inheritance, and strike out on our own. Being ever the loving and faithful One, our God does as his counterpart in the story, and grants us our free will. He sends us on our way: never complaining, never scolding, and ever patient.

I know from personal experience with a prodigal son, that letting go can be the hardest thing in the world to do. You know they are leaving terribly ill-equipped to face the world. They feel they have all the answers when they don't. They exist in a dream world that precludes them from godly, or even rational, thinking. They have often set their faces like flint against any form of authority: spiritual or earthly. You know the reasons they are leaving are the very reasons they should stay and work it out, but you have also come to accept the fact that in their condition you can no longer help them. All further attempts will only serve to widen the chasm already causing gaping wounds in your relationship, and it breaks your heart because you feel so powerless to help them.

When prodigals go astray it is because they have embraced other lovers: the world, idols, their pride, or other gods. So the true and only God must, as the archetype of the father in our story, let go so His rebellious child may be sent to the school of hard knocks for a season.

> And not many days later the younger son gathered everything together and went on a journey into a distant country, and there he squandered his estate with loose living. Now when he had spent everything a severe famine occurred in that country, and he began to be in need. And he went and attached himself to one of the citizens of that country. He sent him into his fields to feed swine. And he longed to fill his stomach with the pods that the swine were eating, but no one gave anything to him *(Luke 15:13-16)*.

We squander so many good things as we wander off on our prodigal experiences. We sacrifice our relationships with both God and people, our focus on the kingdom, our integrity, our money, and even our fidelity. Such foolish pursuits inevitably lead to famine, for without God in our lives the peace we once knew, the security we once knew, and the wisdom and love we once enjoyed abandon us. The source of all that is good withdraws, and we eventually come to be in need. If, at that point, we fail to realize our failings and repent and return to Him, we inevitably go out to look for substitutes.

This search eventually leads to worldly solutions, because without God the world is all that is left to look to for hope, or example. We attach ourselves to just about anything that will satisfy the widening black hole we feel swirling within our souls. As hard as we try to embrace all that the world serves up, satisfaction escapes us. Nothing available for purchase can fill the need. Because the world offers up only imposters, fakes, and weak imitations, we are relegated to *feeding with swine* instead of dining at our Father's table. We fill our lives with every external blessing we can think of to stem the growing starvation we feel inside, but none of these posers give us anything close to what the Father had for us all along.

> But when he came to his senses, he said, "How many of my father's hired men have more than enough bread, but I am dying here with hunger. I will get up and go to my father and say to him, 'Father, I have sinned against heaven, and in your sight. I am no longer worthy to be called your son. Make me as one of your hired men'" (Luke 15:17-19).

When we finally realize the trap pride has set for us, and come to our senses, we realize how sweet our fellowship was at home in the body with our family and our Father. We awaken to the realization that even the least of His children dwell securely in the abundance of His provision. We make a commitment to ourselves to return in repentance and humility to our Maker. We ask Him to grant us what we should have been satisfied with all along. We desire just to be one of His servants, and dwell once again in His presence.

In the pride that drove us from Him, we wanted something more than He was willing to give. We considered ourselves special, above the rest, and worthy to receive our inheritance before the proper time. The patience and self-discipline faith requires was too much to endure, and we chose to seek our own instant gratification instead. We wanted to eat from the forbidden tree and ascend to the heights like the false god who, for a season, became our step-father. When we come to our senses and return to the truth, we realize the foolishness of such thoughts. We desire to again be counted among the least of His servants, and we would seek nothing more if allowed back into the fellowship.

And he got up and came to his father. But while he was still a long way off his father saw him, and felt compassion for him, ran and embraced him, and kissed him *(Luke 15:20)*.

A Step He Won't Take for Us

There is a critical step to restoration here for the prodigal. *He got up and came to his father.* All the intentions of changing—all the words of repentance in the world—mean little more than meaningless repetition if we fail to act upon them. Anyone who has worked with alcoholics, abusers, and drug addicts knows they will over and over again say, "I'm so sorry, I promise this time I'll change." They'll do it with trembling voices and through many tears, before both God and man.

> **All the intentions of changing----all the words of repentance in the world----mean little more than meaningless repetition if we fail to act upon them.**

12-step counselors have learned to recognize this for what it is. They also know how few of these tortured souls really mean it, and are truly ready to act upon their remorse. The sad truth is, God also hears these kinds of empty proclamations all the time from those mired in *practiced* sin patterns. Too often they come without any intention of action attached. Unlike the prodigal, they refuse to get up and go. This young man would have never enjoyed the restoration with his father that the rest of this story is about, had he merely mouthed words of repentance. Yet, this is typically the way we hide behind half-hearted repentant prayers to God. They amount to little more than thoughtless ritual, and we never truly intend to act upon them.

But when we follow words of repentance with deeds of repentance, something incredible happens. As we observe the father's reaction to the son's return, God's grace is masterfully portrayed. Once His lessons of sanctification have sunk in deeply enough that we are willing to act upon, and not merely speak, words of repentance, our Father sees and comes running! However, He will come and get us *only* after this. He will search the horizon, but won't venture beyond *the gate* He put in place to insure a grace He never intended become acceptable to us.

The Father knows we have lessons to learn—sometimes hard lessons. He demands, as He did so many times in the Scriptures, we take a step towards Him in response to the step He took towards us *while we were yet in our sin (Rom. 5:8)*. The only way we will learn is to walk withering deserts alone, with His peace withdrawn. Jesus knows that if He rescued us every time we decided our way was *the* way, we would learn few of wisdom's teachings. What's worse, our ways would become the accepted way for us, because we would come to rightly believe that they work.

In His sanctifying love, God many times has to strike us. But there is another side of the sanctification coin, and that is grace. In His redemptive love, He is locked and loaded to forgive and accept those prodigals who turn back toward home. The son didn't have to come and be announced at the gate, for the father scanned the horizon every minute of every day waiting for his joyous return! No servant had to notify him that his son approached. They found that out as he knocked them aside while running and shouting, "My son…He's back…My son!"

When earthly parents see their sons and daughters go astray, they will call family, friends, school, work, or the authorities in desperate attempts to re-establish communication. They will sit and wait for the phone by the hour for any morsel of information. They will *scan the horizon* through any means necessary to hear news—any news.

A Day of Darkness

I remember driving down a street near my home back in early 2000. As I drove by a park where I had coached little league football, and our family had enjoyed picnics, the sounds of sirens suddenly filled the air. I remember a couple of police cruisers rushing past, as I sat waiting at a stoplight. They headed toward my park. I drove on to work, thinking little of a few sirens. Upon arriving at my destination, I heard the horrid news from everyone as they huddled around their radios, faces creased with the unmistakable masks of disbelief.

The corner I saw the police cruisers rush through was Bowles Avenue and Wadsworth Boulevard. The Park was Clement Park. The city was Littleton, Colorado, and that ominously strange day was

April 20. The high school that stood in view on the other side of the park from my stoplight was Columbine. At that very moment I was driving by, unbeknownst to me, two tortured sons of Satan were on a murderous rampage that shocked the world. Thirteen died that day in a hail of bullets not two miles from my home. It was a day that would live forever in infamy.

At that time Jim, a devoted family man whose kids went to Columbine, and I were in a fellowship group together. His son had played with mine on the little league team I coached. He and his wife were the kind of people who loved being involved in their kids' lives. In fact, Jim's wife was our football team mom. You know the type: wonderful, involved, giving people. Jim and his wife had a son who was one of the first to get out on that fateful morning, and a daughter who was not so fortunate. She was trapped in the science room when the insanity started. She watched a popular teacher bleed to death before her and her classmates' eyes from the cabinets they hid in, and was one of the last ones out.

Jim and his wife first heard about the attack at around 11:30 AM. All of the parents were told to wait for word of their kids' return at either a local elementary school, or the public library at Clement Park. Jim went to the school, and she went to the library. On the evening news that night, film was shown of all of the tortured parents waiting as bus after bus full of kids who made it out safely were ferried in. I only found out a couple of days later that my friend Jim agonized for almost five hours before the last bus came in with their daughter on it. There were other parents there who will never stop waiting and watching for children who will never come home again.

Were they standing by the gate, scanning the horizon? Only a parent can even begin to imagine the sheer terror of those hours—hours that must have seemed like years. Yet this reflects the love God gives us for our children. What a picture this drew for me of God's feelings for all of His prodigals. How much greater a love does He have for His children under the attack of the evil one, lost in deception and sin?

> And the son said to him, "Father, I have sinned against heaven and in your sight. I am no longer worthy to be called your son." But the father said to his slaves, "Quickly bring out the best robe and put it on him, and put a ring on his hand and sandals on his feet. And bring the fattened calf, kill it, and let us eat and be merry, for this son of mine was dead and has come to life again. He was lost and has been found." And they began to be merry *(Luke 15:21-24)*.

Once in the father's presence, it was necessary for the son to *verbalize* his confession, much as it is necessary for us to do in prayer. The son realized his sin, put feet on his repentance, and then verbalized it to the one he had offended as well. Together, the words and actions the son displayed is what the Bible calls bringing forth fruits in accordance with repentance. Then, and only then, did the father give the word to his servants to prepare the feast, and begin the celebration. Why then? Why no feast when the son was still far off? Why, if the father saw the son long before he reached the gate, didn't He tell the servants to prepare the feast ahead of time? I believe that until true, fruit-bearing repentance is both displayed and verbalized, our Father keeps the celebration on hold. He's heard empty words of repentance many times more than any 12-step counselor or therapist, so why call the party before it becomes real?

I believe it is this way with the Communion celebration, for this celebration is all about the dead coming to life and the lost being found. When we are found by God to be in a state of life-restoring repentance, the Calf can be killed on our behalf. When we come as genuinely repentant prodigals to take the Elements that symbolize our Sacrificial Lamb—our Fatted Calf that the Father has prepared for us in the body and blood of Christ—He joyously sets the feast before us! He calls all in the fellowship to join the celebration!

Michael Wolff

Thieves of Grace?

Conversely, I wonder what the father's reaction would have been had the son tried to sneak back, unrepentant and still wandering, to steal the fatted calf from its stall? Yet this is precisely what we do to God when we come to His table as a *thief of grace*—unrepentant, and wanting to steal that which He alone can give. Would there have been a feast prepared in this case for the prodigal, or a trial? Would there have been a celebration, or judgment? Had he refused his own self-examination that led him to repent and return, what would the father's reaction have been then? By partaking unworthily, would he not have been *eating and drinking judgment upon himself*?

> When we come to the Communion table carrying sin that we refuse to confront through both confession and action...We become thieves of grace.

And do we think our Father, who knows all and sees all, and is standing at the gates of heaven daily scanning the horizon for the return of all of His prodigals, does not see our criminal actions? Yet, it is all a part of the rationalization of destructive sin patterns that somehow we think, when we become thieves of grace, He does not see. We think we can offer up empty prayers for forgiveness, and go on living lives that display anything but true repentance, and God's eyes are blinded to it.

When we come to the Communion table carrying un-confessed sin that we refuse to confront, through both confession and action, we become the worst kind of hypocrites. We become thieves of the grace that was prepared before us in the body of Christ at Calvary. We become subject to the severest of God's judgments, as were the Corinthians Paul admonished. It is only because the son examined himself, and came in true repentance, that the table set by the father was the glorious celebration it was. He had turned from the veritable thief of his father's estate, to one who at last understood the father's bounty didn't exist in His possessions, but in His presence. He had been transformed from a thief of grace, to a penitent beneficiary of it. Whereas he was dead, he had now begun to live!

What of the Older Son?

The parable now turns its focus to the older son, who was in the fields working when the prodigal came home. Upon hearing the commotion, he asked one of his servants what was going on. When told a great feast was in the works because his useless younger brother had returned, he became understandably upset. He decided to throw what amounted to a temper tantrum, and refused to go back to the house to join in the festivities. Upon hearing this, his father left the house and went out to find him.

When the two finally got together the older son made a case for his years of faithful service, and asked why his father had never thrown such a celebration on his behalf. The elder son proceeded to list the litany of offenses his younger brother had been guilty of, and wondered why his father was so excited over his return given the history between them. His father then said to him, "My child, you have always been with me, and all that is mine is yours. We had to be merry and rejoice, for this brother of yours was dead and has begun to live. He was lost, and has been found" *(Luke 15:25-32)*.

Ah, the older son, so often relegated to the recycle bin when we hear teaching on this parable. When mentioned, he is often maligned for being such a poor sport. Yet, in his story is a key to understanding even more about God's love than we have seen to this point. It was through a discussion with a friend of mine from church—whom I believed to be an "older son"—that I came to see why mature believers might struggle with my feelings about *The Lost Supper*, as I have seen many do.

The prodigal story is about more than just the less mature struggling to renew a relationship with the Father. It's also about those more mature understanding their role in the Communion process. The prodigal story reflects the struggles of both those Jesus calls *friend*, and those who hear in parables. To focus only upon the younger son is to miss an important point for Jesus' friends. Rather than joining the father in welcoming the younger son back, the older brother forgot the disciple's calling and acted more like a prodigal himself. He displayed pride, and jealousy, and even viewed His good works done for his father as "slaving." Surely, in all of this he was wrong. But at least the older son had tried to be faithful to his father's wishes, and for that the two were treated very differently.

Paul instructed those who were more spiritually mature to come to the aid of their weaker brothers caught up in sin *(Matt. 7:5)*. At the same time, they were to keep an eye on themselves, lest they also be tempted. The older son temporarily forgot both of these instructions. Jesus' goal for any of His children is the creation of disciples who *observe all* He commands *(Matt. 28:19-20)*. This means maturing to the place where they forget about their needs in Christ's love, and minister to the weaker among them.

Paul's relationship with his Lord had reached this plateau. He knew his salvation was assured, and that he was loved and secure in his faith. For him, as for any mature believer, it is all totally and always about finding and saving the lost—inside and outside the walls of the building. This led him to say, "For this reason, brethren, in all our distress and affliction we were comforted about you through your faith. For now we really live, if you stand firm in the Lord" *(1 Thess. 3:8)*. This is what the heart of obedient older sons in the Lord should be. The disciple comes to understand the source and purpose of love, as his becomes the very heart of God. The true disciple goes out not to be served, but to serve, and to be poured out for the objects of its divine affections.

Even though the older son stumbled badly here, as all older sons do from time to time, the father's response to him was quite different than to the younger son. The father reassured the older son that the two had "always been together," and everything the father owned was also the son's. What a perfect picture of Jesus and His children! Just as the younger son's wanderings failed to change the Father's feelings concerning him, so also the older son's wanderings failed to sway His affections. This young man was a trusted co-worker with his father, who just needed to be reminded of it. His position at his father's side remained assured.

In defense of the older brother, however, we need to note the drastic difference in the way the father treated him. In his dealings with the prodigal, the father patiently waited for conviction to run its course. He waited for the son to repent in both word and deed before pursuing him, and would not pursue the prodigal beyond the gate he had set up as the boundary of truth and grace.

Ah, but when the older son became jealous, and began to stray, the father came after him immediately! He *pursued* him to explain his words and actions. The older son was always welcome at the father's table—no prodigal's repentance required. Because of his continual obedience, and practice of earnest faith, good works, and trust, the father wanted him to know unquestionably where he stood.

But did the father go to the younger son, and explain his issues with the older son? While definitely a disciple struggling with perspective at this point—and most assuredly in need of correction—the older brother had become what Jesus would have called a *friend* to his father. Jesus said to His disciples, "You are My friends, if you do what I command you. No longer do I call you slaves, for the slave does not know what his master is doing. But I have called you friends, for all things that I have heard from My Father I have made known to you" *(John 15:15)*.

> **One son was pursued, and the situation explained to him. One was not pursued, and wouldn't have understood had it been explained.**

The father's different reactions in this story to the older and younger sons, is a classic example of the contrast between *friends* and *slaves*. He pursued the older son, as Jesus did His disciples, and all to correct and train them for kingdom service. And while he was overjoyed to see his younger son return, the father wouldn't explain the older son's dilemma to him, knowing he was still a *slave* who couldn't yet fully understand the father's will.

To You Older Sons

If you are one of Jesus' *older sons*: a sinner who strives daily to walk the path of discipleship, take heart! For the most part, Communion's warnings aren't for you. Though the need for repentance never abandons us—and even true disciples need to use the Communion Table to pause and consider—as older sons you are always welcome to the Father's Table! It's about restoring all the prodigals out there who have no compass, and who have lost their way and need to find it again. That focus should take precedence over any personal need for of all of the more mature sons and daughters at Communion.

Paul said, "But we know that the law is good if one uses it lawfully, realizing the fact that law is not made for a righteous man, but for those who are lawless and rebellious" *(1 Tim. 1:9)*. The warnings and laws of Communion are for the hard hearted and self-deceived, who live life daily as prodigals through indulging their destructive sin patterns. They are for those who practice a lifestyle contrary to their high calling, with no intention of repenting other than through lip service. It is about the heart of God who will leave the ninety-nine righteous persons, to go and find the one who has strayed *(Luke 15:4)*. For the older son who strives always to be with the Father, it is about embracing the abundance that is always his, and using this blessed ceremony to minister to the prodigals who need the benefit of his maturity and wisdom.

Older sons join the Father in the work, and take their pleasure in being used by Him to seek and restore the lost. Those who are Jesus' friends abide in His love, and are always a part of what He is doing in His church. However, all older sons need to beware the greatest enemy of all. That is to become trapped in the tentacles of *the shepherd's pride*. Here, the light in us can become darkness, and there is no greater darkness anywhere in Christianity. It is the trap for the mature. It is the trap of thinking we have ever gone beyond the need of correction from the hand of God, through the conviction of His Spirit and the words He has put for us in the mouths of others. If even the most mature ever get to the point of thinking they are beyond their own prodigal experiences, the shepherd's pride is at the door. So even true disciples must beware, and use this time of self-examination as well.

In our efforts to bring back the prodigals at the Lord's Table, we mustn't let pride make prodigals of us. Rather, we should be able to more quickly and easily confront and confess our issues, so we can turn and *remove the speck from our brother's eye (Matt. 7:5)*. It is ever our mandate to see to it that all of God's sons and daughters, younger and older alike receive healing at the Table of truth and grace.

So join in the celebration! Rejoice in Communion's power to restore, heal, and bring about repentance for those prodigals who are ready to return to the fold! Beware the traps set for the more mature, and let Christ's love lead you to act your part as you seek to minister to those less mature. Glory in the fact that He has chosen to explain to you all things He is doing, remain ever-faithful, and thank Him that He has made you His vessel to bear the burdens of others.

VI. TO UNBELIEVERS AND BELIEVERS

An objective examination of Paul's teachings in 1ˢᵗ Corinthians reveals cautions to those both inside and outside the faith. Verses 23-26 could be called the admonitions for the unbeliever, and verses 27-32 the admonitions for the believer. These will be the focus of this chapter. As to the former, Paul warns:

> For I received from the Lord that which I also delivered to you, that the Lord Jesus in the night in which He was betrayed took bread, and when He had given thanks He broke it, and said, "This is My body, which is for you. Do this in remembrance of Me." In the same way He took the cup also after supper, saying, "This cup is the new covenant in My blood. Do this, as often as you drink it, in remembrance of Me." For as often as you eat this bread and drink the cup, you proclaim the Lord's death until He comes *(vs. 23-26)*.

The Greek for *proclaim* in this passage is kataggello. It is not a passive word. It means to affirmatively declare something—to preach or teach it with conviction. When we take Communion, we affirmatively proclaim to all participants gathered that we are believers dedicated to declaring, teaching, and preaching what Paul called the message of *first importance* concerning the gospel: Christ's crucifixion for our sin. Paul said that he would be determined to know nothing else in the life of men than Jesus Christ, *and Him crucified (1 Cor. 2:2)*.

Without acceptance of the work God accomplished on the Cross the rest of the Gospel message meant little, because it was this act that paved the way to salvation that would forever set the God of the Christians apart from all others. Being the only God who offered a workable solution to sin and death made Jesus the only genuine article. At the same time, it rendered all other concocted God's of men's imaginations little more than impotent posers. Proclaiming the Lord's death is first, foremost, and primarily about understanding this act, and accepting its consequences in our lives. Without this understanding, and then believing in and attesting to the Cross in one's life, how could one proclaim the Gospel? How could one who failed to understand this and proclaim it then worthily partake of the Elements of Communion?

And while any unbelievers present must be asked to abstain from the Elements, they should by all means be encouraged to stay and observe. They should feel free to ask questions, while at the same time respecting the seriousness and

> Communion is the best possible environment for the lost to be introduced to real and honest discipleship.

spirit of the proceedings. I have seen souls won to Christ through witnessing *the Lost Supper*. In fact, it is the best possible place for them to see real and honest discipleship they may not have witnessed in God's people before.

Observed properly, Communion is the most authentic setting to witness the power of God working in His people's lives. Here, redeemed sinners confront God and the fellowship as they honestly struggle with their humanness. So by all means, encourage unbelievers to stay, and to keep an open mind to what the Holy Spirit may be saying to them.

Believers can also take a message from these initial passages. For them, there is a message of hope here. The believer can realize anew it is in Christ, and the message of the Cross, they have found a salvation that was available nowhere else. In the shedding of His blood, and the brokenness of His body, is the grace of the crucified Son so ready, willing, and able to restore and renew them for the battle, until they meet again at His Table. Here we find another similarity between the 12-step creed and biblical Communion:

> We admitted we were powerless over [our sinful practices]—that our lives had become unmanageable…

> We made a decision to turn our will and our lives over
> to the care of God. [words in brackets are mine] 12

At the Table of the Lord, believers admit they are powerless over sinful practices, and make decisions to turn their will and their lives over to His care. We are reminded *here* that our lives had become totally unmanageable before Jesus suffered the Cross to set us free. We are reminded *here* that Jesus alone holds salvation in His hands, and that His forgiveness is ever available to the repentant believer.

Paul's Message to Believers

But now the unbeliever's warning, and the believer's reassurance, of verses 23-26 take a turn that has become too discomforting for most modern administrators to even read, much less effectively teach and apply. For here Paul begins cautioning the believer, and that is something rarely done in this age of grace without command:

> "Therefore whoever eats the bread or drinks the cup of the Lord in an unworthy manner, shall be guilty of the body and blood of the Lord. But let a man examine himself, and so let him eat of the bread and drink of the cup. For he who eats and drinks, eats and drinks judgment to himself if he does not judge the body rightly. For this reason many among you are weak and sick, and a number sleep" *(vs. 27-30)*.

Two points here confirm this portion of the Communion instruction is specifically targeting believers. The first is Paul's use of the word *sleep*. Matthew 27 and John 11 contain this same word [Greek: koimesis or koimao, which means to lie down and sleep]. It is used only in reference to the physical passing of the flesh of *believers*. Jesus said that if we believed in Him, though our bodies would suffer decay and cease to function, our souls and spirits would never die *(John 11:25-26)*. Therefore, the need for two separate words to describe *death*: one that refers to the passing of the flesh only of believers, and one that refers to the death—body and soul—of unbelievers.

When the Bible refers to the cessation of life of an unbeliever, the word used is nekros [in the Greek: literal death]. Were God's children to suffer the same fate in bodily death as those who have refused Him, then Jesus would have died for nothing. If Paul were addressing the position of unbelievers, as he is in verses 23-26, this word would be nekros, and not koimesis. By saying many in Corinth had fallen asleep as a result of their superficial observances of the Lord's Table, Paul is saying that they had actually died in the flesh.

This was a time in the history of Christ's church where people did physically perish because of sin [see the story of Annas and Sapphira in Acts 5]. Messing around with hypocrisy wasn't a safe thing to do, particularly at this most holy of ceremonies. While we see little in the physical realm like this occurring today, do we not find many in the church who are *spiritually* weak, sick, and asleep? Oh yes, God's judgments for unworthily partaking of Communion are alive and well! The story may be old, but the power of the God who watches over it is still very, very real.

In *Velvet Elvis*, Rob Bell says this about the relevance of those old stories to ours of today:

> This is why the Bible is still so powerful: these ancient stories are our stories. These stories are reflective of how things are. And this is why the Bible loses its power for so many communities. They fall into the trap of thinking that the Bible is just about things that happened a long time ago. 13

This is perhaps nowhere truer than concerns our contemporary views of Communion, and the power it still contains. The consequences of weakness, sickness, and sleep we see spiritually manifesting themselves—not only in the body of individuals, but also in the body-corporate of the church—is

> **The consequences of weakness, sickness, and sleep we see manifested spiritually in the church, are due largely to our inability to properly judge ourselves within the body.**

due largely to our refusal to enter in to the self-examination process. It comes through refusing to judge ourselves during improperly administered and observed Communion ceremonies.

The second proof that Paul is targeting the saved in these latter verses of his Communion instruction revolves around the issue of internal judgment by the fellowship. Paul says that if we judged *ourselves* rightly, we would not be judged. But *when* we are judged, we are disciplined by the Lord so we won't be condemned along with the world *(vs. 31-32)*. In another instruction to the Corinthians, Paul admonishes the Corinthians for allowing immoral men to remain a part of the fellowship. He tells them to refuse to associate with any such person who claims to be a brother. Then he says, "For what have I to do with judging outsiders? Do you not judge those who are within the church? But those who are outside God judges, therefore, remove the wicked man from among yourselves" *(1 Cor. 5:13)*.

Paul makes a clear distinction between those we in the church *should* judge, and those we should not. He says that we have nothing to do with judging outsiders [unbelievers], but then asked the Corinthians why they refused to judge those who were in the fellowship. To reiterate, the reason we are to judge within the body of Christ, is to avoid being condemned along with the world. Who is *the world* Paul refers to here, if not those outside the church?

If Paul were not speaking here specifically to believers, why would this issue of judgment come up at all? If we are not to judge those outside the body, and yet he is calling for judgment among those gathered, who could he possibly be referring to other than believers? There is one judgment for the believer and another judgment for the unbeliever.

I would ask all of our religious teachers, "If Communion is all about grace, as you believe and teach, please explain all of this talk about judging *ourselves* found in Paul's letters to the Corinthians?"

Being Righteously Judgmental

As the world calls out, "Live and let live…don't be judgmental and narrow-minded…do your own thing," we in the church are to live by a very different standard—and this because God judges us by a different standard. Those who live in darkness, and those who are supposed to be dwelling in light, rightly should be judged accordingly.

Inasmuch as Paul delivers such a clear warning for those who believe in the Lord Jesus Christ to be *righteously* judgmental among their own members, what does it mean? How does that fit into the Communion environment? Inasmuch as the self-deceived believer will often play the "You're-judging-me" card as a first line of defense, we need to know how to respond with a defense that dismantles their argument.

Jesus had the perfect response to this in John 12: "He who rejects Me, and does not receive My sayings, has one who judges him. The word I spoke is what will judge him at the last day." The prophet Zechariah said, "These are the things which you should do: speak the truth to one another, and judge with truth and judgment for peace in your gates" *(Zech. 8:16)*. When we admonish one another in a spirit of Christ's love, and with biblical truth and doctrine, we must refuse to recoil when accused of being judgmental. Our words aren't judging the unrepentant sinner, but rather the words of God Himself are doing the convicting. It is *always* the right thing to confront a self-deceived brother or sister with the truth of God's Word, as long as we do it at the right place and time, in a spirit of love, and with the hope of reconciliation.

We will never know true peace within the church until we learn to enter into righteous judgment with one another. The Word of God is designed to pierce through the denials and rationalizations of the self-deceived. Speaking it in truth will take the focus off of you, where they are desperately trying to keep it so they don't have to face their sin. It will place that focus on the One who has the power to shatter their darkness, and the One with whom they cannot argue.

However we are led to go about it, righteous judgment is a critical process to the health of the body. Peter said that it was time for judgment to begin with the household of God *(1 Pet. 4:17)*. As previously discussed Matthew 18:15-18 proceeds from one brother judging another, to two or more entering in, to the body-corporate judging him. In another passage from *The Message* in 1st Corinthians 5, Paul says:

> I'm not responsible for what the outsiders do, but don't we have some responsibility for those within our community of believers? God decides on the outsiders, but we need to decide when our brothers and sisters are out of line and, if necessary, clean house! [14]

Louis Berkhof, in his book *Systematic Theology*, relates the need for the church to police herself concerning allowing the impenitent at the Table:

> It is possible that [the church] occasionally admits hypocrites to the privileges of full Communion, but such persons in par-taking of the Lord's Supper will only eat and drink judgment upon themselves. And if their unbelief and ungodliness becomes evident, the church will have to exclude them by the proper administration of church discipline. The holiness of the church and of the sacrament must be safeguarded. 15

Much of what the Bible teaches about the conduct of believers begins with righteous judgment. We in the church *are* to judge ourselves, both personally and as a body. It is critical to the sanctification of the body-corporate. We are to approach this process as diligent workmen who do not need to be ashamed, because we handle the truth accurately *(2 Tim. 2:15)*, and in a spirit of gentleness, with the goal of restoring our confused and less mature brothers *(Gal. 6:1)*.

Righteous judgment is a delicate balance of confrontation and encouragement. It is the balance that Christ Himself displayed constantly as Savior and Judge. We must open the eyes of our deluded members without unrighteous judgment or false piety, and this is precisely why God gave us this ceremony.

Throughout history, God has provided prophets for His people. Each of them has proclaimed loudly and single-mindedly, "Turn around, repent, and amend your ways or the judgment of Him who is faithful and true is coming upon you." It's our choice: judge ourselves within the fellowship, or have it brought down upon us. Either way, judgment of hypocrites, and those practicing worldliness, is assured by a holy God zealous over His own legacy.

> **It's our choice: judge ourselves within the fellowship, or incur judgment from above.**

If we would but utilize the gift of Communion to judge ourselves regularly, through objective individual and corporate self-examination, we wouldn't have to face the more costly option of having it forced upon us. It is always true that consequences are fewer, and less-severe, when we act upon small problems before they turn in to large ones. When God's hand becomes heavy because we refuse to avail ourselves of repentance through this regular self-examination process, the price is always much higher for the same lesson.

Ray Pritchard, in this entry in Lawrence Kimbrough's marvelous compilation of devotionals, *Men of Character*, says:

> Just remember, when it comes to solving problems the first price you pay is always the cheapest. We ignore problems, hoping they will go away, but that rarely happens. And the price of solving them goes up, not down. Problems never get better when you ignore them. You may think you love someone too much to say anything. No, if you really love him you would speak the truth. You would speak it in love, but you would speak the truth he needed to hear. 16

…and Bonhoeffer:

> But since sin must come to light some time, it is better that it happens today between me and my brother, rather than on the last day in the piercing light of the final judgment. It is a mercy that we can confess our sins to a brother. Such grace spares us the terrors of the last judgment. 17

If those shepherding the Lord's Table will leave no doubt that there are warnings to both believers and unbelievers here, the wonderful opportunity to bring up and then administer righteous judgment within the body will be made available to them. Molehills will stop becoming mountains, and regular maintenance will supplant crises management. The burden of putting God's judgment off that is heavy, will be replaced by the yoke of regular maintenance that is light.

The unbelievers' instruction here is simple. They don't need to discern where deception, cover-up, and superficiality may exist. They only need to think about placing their faith in Jesus Christ or not. For believers, the self-examination process can be much more complicated, and much more demanding. That is why we come together in this divinely inspired ceremony, custom-tailored to help believers confront the scrutiny and truth of God's dismantling convictions, and act upon them.

Communion was given to us so we wouldn't be judged along with the world. We must use it to take seriously his warnings to us, judge righteously among ourselves, and let this miraculous gift fulfill its cleansing, healing purpose. No matter how uncomfortable the work of policing within the body is, it will be far preferable to the policing that will come from above if we fail.

VII. RECOGNIZING SIN

Something within us must die, and we must be the executioners. We are not to let it live while we try to behave better...We are to grab it by the neck and throttle it, and throttle it again every time it shows up...And if he [it] doesn't stay dead, we must shoot him again, then beat him, then tie him down in the sand under a hot desert sun, turn loose an army of red ants on his body and walk away without sympathy. 18

The *something that must die* at any table that speaks of Holy Communion is the flesh. It is the tenaciousness of our sinful nature that led Jesus to command us to deny ourselves, and take up our crosses *daily (Luke 9:32)*. The *he* that Dr. Crabb refers to is Satan: the one whose own self-deceptive nature dictates that he will never, this side of his final judgment, believe that he can possibly lose this fight. Therefore, no matter how many times you throttle him, and throttle him again, he will get up and keep right on coming.

It, and he, are not to be understood or allowed to succeed, but rather to be battled decisively with every weapon available. We must take a proactive role in their execution! This is not a battle God will take on for us alone, but one He will joyously join in with us as we take up His full armor and go forth in endurance and faith.

Through capitalizing on our *thorns in the flesh*, Satan erects roadblocks between us and God. Through Communion, God seeks to expose those roadblocks to us. Regular self-exams provide for us an enduring understanding of the Devil and his plots through a constantly renewed and cleansed relationship with Jesus. This regular cleansing makes us ready for that next step He always has waiting for His children who seek to mature in that relationship. Michael Wells says of this:

> The message of losing all to gain Him can be an unpleasant message, and it can be an unwelcome discovery that a deeper revelation of flesh is necessary before a deeper revelation of Him can occur. 19

While it may sound strange to seek a deeper revelation of the flesh, the beginning of a cure for any disease is found in a revelation of the problem in the mind of the deceived.

To discuss warnings about taking the Table in possibly self-destructive ways without helping people through the process of a deeper revelation of flesh, would be a little like telling someone a bridge is out on a dark, stormy night without telling them where. People asked to confront sin who have been unaccustomed to it are often confused, because the very nature of superficiality and self-deception is to think we don't have a problem when in fact we do.

> **A good starting point for discovering some basics of self-deception can be found in examining God's first commandment, and Satan's favorite lie.**

When participant's eyes are reopened to specific areas of sin in their lives, they will be better able to deal with them. While there are many, many sinful desires and habits we could fill volumes with, a good starting point for discovering some basics of self-deception and stalled spiritual growth can be found in examining God's first commandment, and Satan's favorite lie.

The Foundations of Sin

The first and foremost command according to Jesus is, "Love the Lord your God with all your heart, soul, mind, and strength. And love your neighbor as yourself" *(Matt. 22)*. Satan's favorite lie is contained in the first book of the Bible, and also one of the last. This demonstrates the fact that through time it has never changed, perhaps because it works so well. The old adage, "If it isn't broken, don't fix it" would seem to apply. Weaving Genesis 3:6 and 1st John 2:16 together, we find that the master-deceiver has always fed upon *the lust of the flesh* [the fruit good for food], *the lust of the eyes* [a delight to the eyes] and *the boastful pride of life* [desirability to make one wise]. From these arise a polluted spring from which most other areas of subsequent sin gush forth.

Peter said, "And I consider it right, as long as I am in this earthly dwelling, to stir you up by way of *reminder*" *(2 Pet. 3:1)*. He understood the nature of the beast, and that continued attacks required continued reminders to his people, because of Satan's tenaciousness and ability to lull us to sleep. Speaking God's Word that will slowly stir up the human spirit by bringing conviction of sin, and open the doors to the sanctifying work Communion is all about. Those walls of rationalized and denied sin-addictions will eventually begin to crack and crumble under the withering blows of God's double-edged sword, but leaders of God's people must be as tenacious in stirring up this conviction as Satan is in numbing it down.

Genesis 3 and 1st John 2 lead us to the following foundations of sin. Please keep in mind I am not saying we must be perfect to come to the Lord's Table, nor do we need to have conquered all of our demons. What we do need to do is realize where we have been deceived into thinking habitual sin patterns are okay, and be willing to confess them and take up the fight anew:

- ✦ Wrong priorities: The Great Commandment, Matthew 10:37-39, and Colossians 1:16-18, reveal the absolute truth that Jesus Christ needs to be number one in our lives. Any possessions or desires placed above following Him become idols, which will keep us from true fellowship with Him. Some typical idols would be job, material possessions, coveting what others have, or any other thing or positions which may be the primary focus of one's desires. Participants need to examine themselves in the light of Christ's probing question to Peter, "Do you love me more than these" *(John 21:15)*, to see if anything in their lives comes before their desire for a disciple's relationship with Him. There can be absolutely nothing one deems more important than his or her walk with Jesus as they come before the Altar.

- ✦ Spirit of unforgiveness: 2 Corinthians 2:10-11, Mark 11:25-

26, and Colossians 3:13, deal with refusal to forgive anyone of *any* transgression. Such harbored resentment stands flatly in opposition to the Great Commandment to *love our neighbor.* The Lord says He will refuse His forgiveness to anyone who likewise refuses to forgive their brothers and sisters *(Matt. 18).* To the Lord's Table, of all places, we need to come forgiving *and* forgiven. This sort of transgression rears its ugly head often in our modern society, within the dysfunction of our family units. The problem of family members holding entrenched, long-standing feelings of ill-will is rampant in our culture of ignored, discarded, and abusive family relationships.

One suffering from this affliction, whatever the source, needs to be encouraged to take a stand against hateful thoughts and harbored grudges, for this is what is meant by *letting the sun set on our anger (Eph. 4:26).* We must refuse it a place setting at the Lord's Table. Family or not, they are our neighbors, and to love them we must first forgive them.

✦ Lust of the flesh and of the eyes: Matthew 5:27-28, and 1st Corinthians 6:18, cover this one. Lust, the man killer—the one sin that Paul tells us to *flee.* Lust is the one that will win every time unless we remove its catalysts entirely from our lives. This transgression, a sin which we are not to even attempt to stand toe-to-toe against, is absolutely pervasive in its enslavement of believers today. Pornography's overwhelming availability is making it a growing problem for everyone in this world.

This is the one that got to David: the man who had a *heart after God's own.* It got to Solomon: *the wisest man who ever lived.* In this world of pornographic magazines, cable television, and the internet, this beast is all-too-easily indulged. Even the purest of heart and the most knowledgeable in the Scriptures are no match if they don't turn tail and run for their lives!

Addictions of all kinds must be lain upon the altar of the Lord, and those caught in their death grip challenged to confess. If they don't, they will never be free from the guilt, the shame, and all of the corresponding collateral damage and consequences addictions bring. They can only be dealt with through utter reliance on the power of the Spirit, and regular accountability with others in the body. Simply stated, if one harbors any kind of un-confessed closet addiction they are unwilling to confront, they are unworthy to partake of the Elements.

- Hard-Heartedness: Ah, the boastful pride of life—the forbidden fruit that we desire to *make us wise*. John 9:39-41, Romans 2:4-5, and Numbers 15:30-31, reveal the dangers of a hard heart. This is the most all-encompassing sin waiting to snare even the mature child of God. Pride will, more often than not, be the one that true disciples at the Communion Table will be struggling with. Hard-heartedness is an umbrella for most of all sin. It entails a refusal to allow the Holy Spirit to work in our lives, because we think we have the truth figured out. It is the arrogance that comes with thinking the Holy Spirit has nothing left to teach us in any one given area of life. Pride is the sin of the Pharisees. Pride is the reason they refused to be taught anything by Jesus, even though they should have been the first to have recognized Him. Pride is a disease that can put us on the thinnest of ice with our God.

Anyone who has become hardened to their sin, to the point that they no longer feel the need to repent [a particularly grievous condition the Scriptures call *lawlessness*] is walking on shaky ground indeed. There is absolutely no place for this impenitent attitude at the Table, because to allow one with a hard heart to partake. It can only lead to further hardening and self-deception. This is what is so dangerous about the toothless ceremonies modern religion largely presides over. Not only are sin-addictions that lead to hard hearts allowed to continue on unopposed, but these destructive patterns are even reinforced through non-reflective ritualistic participation.

By proclaiming false grace at the Table of the Lord, we in essence say to the hard-hearted, "It's okay. Go ahead and lead a double life. Cheat on your wife, enmesh yourself hopelessly in all forms of addictions, and turn your neighbors and friends away from Jesus with your hypocrisies. You can always come here, and be forgiven without any challenge to your lifestyle whatsoever."

No!!! Communion was created to be the hard-heart-buster! God gave us this ceremony to constantly remind us of the intrepid monster within each of us that is our pride. This one traps us even in the *righteous* deeds that we do. Through confession and repentance, Communion gives us the opportunity to humble ourselves before God and His fellowship on a regular basis.

✦ Superficiality: One of the greatest hindrances to personal spiritual growth is the self-deception of superficiality. Like the Laodiceans *(Rev. 3)*, we think we practice a lifestyle we do not. We believe we follow Christ, when our lifestyle practices say anything but. Depending upon the polling numbers you choose to believe, somewhere between 85 - 90 percent of Americans *believe* they are Christian. I wonder what that number would be if the question was amended to ask, "Are you a disciple of Jesus?" Can you even imagine how different this culture would look were 85 - 90 percent of our entire population *practicing* followers of Jesus Christ? Can you imagine if the same was true, among even the far smaller number of those going to church on a regular basis?

> Superficiality means practicing a lifestyle that we are not—thinking in our minds we are following Christ, when in practice we are not.

The simple truth is that we have become a nation that thinks it follows God, but the evidence proves otherwise. We have become a church with the same problem. Our numbers concerning divorce, alcoholism, family dysfunction, etc., rival those among unbelievers. The vast majority of those who think they are Christ-followers today have no daily meditations, reach out to no one in evangelism or service, are as materialistic as any outside the faith, are functionally illiterate in their knowledge of the Scriptures, and don't hold to Biblical world views.

One tried and tested way to discern the existence of superficiality is to simply review schedules and financial expenditures. How people spend their time and money is the truest test of what's in their hearts. Where our earthly treasure is, our hearts also are *(Matt. 6:21)*. Do our schedules regularly include time with God, time in fellowship, and time in kingdom pursuits? Who in our lives are we evangelizing, discipling, or serving in the love of Christ? Are there any entries in there to go to the church for something other than Sunday services? Are there times to be Good Samaritans to the needy outside the church? Are there times to do some talking or listening over a cup of coffee with a hurting friend?

We can have all knowledge, and give our bodies to be burned according to Paul, yet without love it is nothing but a bunch of religious *noise* to those looking on. If the answer to these questions contradicts what their schedules reveal, superficiality exists. Jesus heard a lot of *noise* from the Laodiceans, but what He saw in the evidence of their works literally sickened Him.

And what about the checkbook? This too is a pervasive issue in our modern American society, as the demand that a man provide for his family has been twisted beyond any recognition of biblical constraints. While Paul did say that a man who does not provide for his own household is worse than an unbeliever *(Tit. 5:8)*, that did not mean he was to work himself to death to store up treasures on earth in the form of a comfortable retirement, funds to send the kids to the best colleges, and keeping up with the Jones's purchases of the latest toys and luxury items *(Matt. 6:19)*. He did not mean a man is to make money his master *(Matt. 6:24)*, as he proves by spending 50-60 hours per week working for earthly gain, yet having no time to spend tilling the fields for the kingdom of heaven.

Are participants tithing regularly, and giving to something other than their church? Do they ever give to anyone without demanding a tax deduction for themselves? Do they spend all the extra funds they have on their own desires? Do they trust in their money, or in God? Really? People can easily deceive themselves into thinking they are putting God first, but it's hard to argue with the schedule and checkbook.

Living in Sin

Paul told us to *run* from immorality *(1 Corinthians 6:18)*, and James instructed us to submit to God and to *resist* the Devil by, among other things, cleansing our hands *(James 4:7)*. Breaking free from the strongholds of sin Satan has been able to secure in our lives many times means dealing with our physical environment, as much as our spiritual condition. Within any of the above afflictions we can exacerbate our situation, and make it many times more difficult to escape, if we do not pay heed to our environment as well as our thoughts.

Not to single out homosexuality, but it is a prime example to most trapped in its lifestyle of what is meant by "living in sin." If a homosexual refuses to break off a steady relationship, the chances of breaking free of the sinful spiritual condition is reduced dramatically, much as it would be were an alcoholic living in a bar or liquor store. The same would be true of those living in an adulterous or pre-marital sexual relationship, or a porn addict living in an X-rated movie house or adult magazine store.

I remember a famous Christian basketball star in Denver, who later went on to coach the Nuggets. He had temper and language issues he admitted to, as he was out speaking and teaching at Christian functions during the day. These shortcomings would then be on display for all to see by night, as he ranted, raved, and threw around expletives like so much dust in the wind before thousands watching the games on television. He truly loved the game, and loved coaching, but it put him in a position where his physical environment enflamed his sinful spiritual condition, and made him look to the eyes of all watching like the world's biggest hypocrite. He finally stepped down when one of his tirades with a heckling fan became racial in nature, and the media attention forced him to retire.

Recognizing sin many times means having to recognize we need to change very practical things about the way we are living, and to remove from our lives harmful practices or people that enflame our sinful desires. If we refuse to do that, we put ourselves in environments where it becomes nearly impossible to even begin dealing with our spiritual condition. The Bible calls us to forsake our worldly circumstances, and to follow Jesus. How difficult would it have been for Matthew to continue as a tax-collector for Rome, and yet tell people he was a disciple of Christ? How difficult would it have been for Paul to continue dragging Christians from their churches and homes, many times to be persecuted or even killed by the Jews, and be known as the great Apostle he became?

If a participant in the Communion ceremony is unwilling to consider changing physical circumstances like the ones described above, the chances for any true repentance is, at best, minimal. Such a person must be admonished to abstain for their own good, until such time as they are willing to submit to God's call to follow Him in a more realistic way. If the homosexual is willing to break off the regular relationship, and yet on occasion stumbles into a homosexual affair, it is a far different thing than daily living in the affair. Can any of us say we do not stumble into sinful affairs of one kind or another? Of course not, for that would be saying we were "without sin," and that would make us the worst of liars.

The Lord's Table is the place for all believers who stumble occasionally into sin to come, be cleansed, and start anew. If those trapped in physical environments are willing to take the often drastic, self-sacrificing steps to extricate themselves, they are to be encouraged, applauded, and welcomed on-board, for they have made a paradigm shift from "living in sin," to being repentant sinners who sometimes stumble and fall.

Jesus Always Does His Part

God is not to be blamed when believers fail to mature in their faith by becoming trapped in destructive sin patterns. The door to repentance is always open. More than that, Peter speaks of the omnipotent power God has given us that supplies

> **Jesus will always heal our past if we will but let Him come in. He will always lead us into the future if we will but follow Him.**

everything we need to pursue godly lives *(2nd Pet.1)*. Jesus is the Author *and* Perfecter of our faith, and is always proactive in our experience. He has done His part to prove everything we need to attain to maturity is fully available in His Spirit. The only thing that can possibly hinder this pro-activity is us presenting an indifferent heart and a deaf ear.

Jesus will always respond when we recognize our transgressions, open the door to the past and let Him come in to heal it. The Good Shepherd will always go before us if we will but follow Him into the future. Communion concerns leaving a past we cannot change in God's hands by recognizing and confessing our sin, and then moving into a future spiritually unimpeded. Again, from Michael Wells:

> The enemy cannot start an invasion without having a foothold in the flesh. I used to believe that a great struggle with the enemy revealed a great heart for God, when actually a great struggle with the enemy reveals a wrong heart. It reveals flesh. It reveals a stronghold. Christ's struggle with Satan did not last for days or even hours, since there was nothing there that found the temptation appealing. [20]

We must give Satan a foothold for him to have power over us, and inasmuch as we are sinful people he will always find places and ways to attack us. However, those attacks will be far more powerful and lasting if we fail to recognize our sins through the opportunities afforded us at the Table. Our spiritual growth will certainly be impeded or come to a halt altogether, as sins that could have been dealt with become practices. When we take lack of growth and dismiss it, and become apathetic or numb to it, superficiality will find its perfect growth culture.

The footholds we give to the flesh must be grabbed by the neck and throttled, and throttled again every time they show up. And they will show up. Jesus stands ready to do His part, every time and without fail. He will convict us, empower us to confess, forgive us, clean us up, set us back on our feet, and cheer us on every time we honor the reason for the Table. Communion has been given to so we can recognize Satan's footholds and free ourselves.

Confession of sinful patterns is much better facilitated if administrators encourage an open and honest look by all into sinful and superficial living. When the Spirit is invited through the Communion setting into a group of believers to do His work, you will be amazed at the power of the results. Opening the door to His conviction and leading will be aided greatly if the group is given direction through teaching and discussion that helps them sort out together where buried and denied sin may hide. Souls asleep to cover-ups must be stirred up through reminder, or they will remain lost in a stormy sea of confusion with no lighthouse to illumine the path of redemption.

VIII. THE SOMA: THE BODY OF CHRIST

There is very little God cares more about than preparing His bride-in-waiting. He will admonish, teach, correct, and train her relentlessly until that glorious day when she stands by His side in heaven, fully united with Him for eternity. He will spare no rod to protect her from enemies, both from without and within. Conversely, He will forego no effort to display His love for those after His own heart, who expend themselves daily for her perpetuation and edification. There are very few topics that the New Testament spends more time on than our place in, our conduct towards, and our involvement with the body-corporate [His church].

I believe Paul weaved into his Communion instruction the way for the church to realize and maintain these lofty goals, for at His Table God convicts those who have become neutralized in their faith to recognize how they hinder the body. It is also there that He leads them back to productivity. Then they can begin to fulfill their unique role for the bride's benefit. They can begin to contribute their unique gifts for the edification of the fellowship, rather than living for themselves on the sidelines, as spectators of the great adventure.

The Book of Fellowship

It is no mere coincidence that Paul's Communion instructions are found immersed in the context of 1st Corinthians. An overview of this book reveals that it is *the* New Testament treatise dealing with the body of Christ, to wit:

+ Chapters one and three contain instructions and warnings concerning divisions in the body.
+ Chapter five concerns how to administer church discipline, and the absolute mandate we have to be righteously judgmental

within the body.
- ✦ Chapter six includes Paul's lament over lawsuits in the body.
- ✦ Chapters eight and ten discuss our liberties in, and causing stumbling amongst the members of, the body.
- ✦ Chapters ten and eleven focus on the maintenance of the members of the body, and thus the body itself, through proper participation in the Holy Communion.
- ✦ Chapter eleven discusses the place of man and woman in the body.
- ✦ Chapters twelve through fourteen provide extensive teaching on use and abuse of spiritual gifts in the body, and,
- ✦ Chapter sixteen speaks of financial support of the body.

There is no other book in the New Testament where such focus is placed on the subject of the body-corporate of Christ. It follows, then, that Communion would deal not only with the individual's place with Christ, but also his place within the body. It is to this end that Paul speaks of judging *the body* rightly in his instruction.

For a long time, I struggled with what Paul meant by this. As I prayed and continued my studies, I was led to look at the believer's place from more than one perspective. There is a concept that can be revelatory to our understanding of our role in the body of Christ in 1st Corinthians 10 and 11. However, before I begin with this, I am reminded of something Paul said when discussing marriage. He felt he had no direct command from the Lord, but also said he felt he was with the Spirit in his teaching. Of the balance of my perspective in this book, I am at peace with my theology, and know that it can be defended. However, in this chapter I am going to enter in to some speculation, albeit I pray well-reasoned speculation. I urge you, therefore, to take some advice from John, and test the spirits here to see whether they are from God *(1 John 4:1)*.

The Soma: The Body of Christ

I believe one of the chief issues participants should consider within the self-examination process revolves around the word *body* [Greek: soma]. Without fully grasping the meaning of this word, we can believe we are guilty of sinning only against Christ's sacrifice on the Cross—*His* body alone—by unworthily partaking of the Elements. To believe this is to perhaps understand only part of the truth. The physical body is only part of the Greek definition for soma. This word also means the body as a whole: a closely united group of any size that molds into one society. While there could be other interpretations to this passage, there is strong evidence that Paul wasn't talking about Christ's literal body here, as he was in earlier passages. He very well could have been speaking of the church!

> There is strong evidence that Paul wasn't talking just about Christ's literal body here. He was speaking of the church!

In 1st Corinthians 10, Paul gives us a preamble to the Communion teaching immediately to follow: "Is not the cup of blessing which we bless a sharing in the blood of Christ? Is not the bread which we break a sharing in the body of Christ? Since there is one bread, we who are many are one body, for we all partake of the one bread" *(1 Cor. 10:17)*. Reviewing this passage, we could say the first *soma* referred to is the body of Christ Himself, because it is tied directly to His blood. Proceeding on to the second reference, we see that Paul compares Christ's body—standing alone now as the bread—to His body-corporate, through our sharing together in its breaking.

It is through Christ's broken body [*His* soma] that we can now all be one body [the *church* soma] in the sharing of that sacrifice. In doing this, Paul makes the body of Christ-personal that we participate in, the same as the body of Christ-corporate that we likewise participate in. The broken physical body becomes the food of the unified church body that was born of the sacrifice we are to remember at the Communion Table.

If this were the only evidence of the soma meaning two different things, my theories could be easily debated. However, Paul refers the two somas *again* in the Communion instructions themselves. In verses 27 and 28 of 1st Corinthians 11, Paul uses the body and blood of the Lord together, thus signifying Christ's personal sacrifice. However, in verse 29 Paul's message once again changes. Notice here the blood is missing, and the body is mentioned alone. Why would Paul, who had been so careful up to this point to focus on the body and blood together, remove the blood from the text here?

Just as he did in chapter 10, he starts with the body and blood and then leaves the blood out—thereby transforming the meaning of soma from body-personal to something else. I believe he removed the blood here because he was no longer referring to the body *and* blood of the Lord. Paul's focus had switched to the body-corporate in *both* of these passages. Christ's body, when it becomes independent of His blood, becomes His body on earth: the church.

There could only be three options for the use of the word *body* in these verses: 1) the physical body of Christ, 2) the physical body of the participant, or, 3) the body-corporate of the church. Due to the absence of the blood—and the impossibility of judging the physical body of Christ [inasmuch as He was perfect and never sinned]—we can eliminate the first option. The second option alone falls short as well, because we know our physical body is part of the flesh, and thus totally sinful. When most believers fall into sin it is because they're souls [mind, will, and emotions] are self-deceived, rather than failing to understand the inherent sinfulness of their flesh. If we had to clean up the flesh to be worthy to partake of Communion, none of us would ever qualify.

I believe the best answer lies in the combination of the second and third options. Given the focus of 1st Corinthians being on the body, along with the two verses just discussed, to say Paul is speaking of judging our body-personal, and how it contributes to the body-corporate, would be a plausible argument.

Also in 1st Corinthians (chapter 12), we find an unhealthy model of the individual's impact on the collective: "When one member of the body suffers, all members suffer with it." Paul also describes the healthy model in Ephesians 4: "We are to grow up in all aspects into Him who is the head, even Christ, from whom the whole body being fitted and held together by that which every joint supplies according to the proper working of each individual part, causing the growth of the body for the building up of itself in love." The cumulative message of Paul to the Corinthians, indicates the proper function coming from both somas—personal and corporate—working in harmony.

Sins of Omission and Commission

The focus up to now has been upon sin of *commission*. That is, sin we commit through action or spoken word. Yet when it comes to the soma, where most fall the hardest is not through acts of commission, but rather acts of *omission*. These are gifts we fail to discover, develop, and deploy—good deeds we fail to do, the ministries we fail to fulfill, or words left unspoken that should have been said. They are all of the opportunities to bear fruit in this

> When it comes to the soma, our self-examination should include whether or not we are harming the fellowship by our acts of *omission* more than those of commission.

world God provides that we allow to pass by without corresponding actions on our part. If Paul is speaking of the church in his use of soma in 1st Corinthians, shouldn't our self-examination include reflection upon whether or not we contribute to the health of the body, as well as our personal walks of faith?

Think of it this way: if one member of the body is mired in unrepentant sin, and has become apathetic, unproductive, or lives in a state of self-deceived superficiality, the entire body becomes proportionately less effective. And if we refuse to *proactively* do the deeds that Jesus tells us to do, do we not also weaken the body? According to 1st Corinthians 12, those who suffer cause the whole body suffer with them. The body becomes more susceptible to weakness, sickness, and sleep than it would be with the healthy contribution of each and every member. It stands to reason, then, that if enough members are individually impaired, the entire body would take on those same characteristics.

Brian Hathaway says this in *Beyond Renewal*, his book that focuses on bringing the Kingdom of God into the church:

> A radical change within the life of each individual is the starting point for permanent change in people and society. The Kingdom rule of God must commence in the lives of individuals if it is to effectively extend into and impact all areas of society [and the church]. [Words in parenthesis mine] 21

John Eldredge follows suit in *Wild at Heart*:

> There is no other man who can replace you in your life, in the arena you've been called to. If you leave your place in line, it will remain empty. No one else can be who you are meant to be. 22

There are no unimportant members in the fellowship of the saints—no members we can afford to leave in a perpetual state of immaturity, if the soma is going to fully fulfill her mandate on this earth. God knew that any fellowship, no matter the size, would function only as well as the sum of its parts did. Remove the $5.00 oil filter from a $350,000 Rolls Royce and, even if every other part is functioning perfectly, a magnificent automobile will become a glorified paperweight in very short order.

As a part of our Communion observance, we need to examine acts we are *omitting* as well as those we are *committing*, for merely repenting of personal sin does not necessarily mean proactively moving forward in making a positive contribution to others. James spoke of a *positive* way to deal with sin—the other side of the repentance coin: "My brethren, if any among you strays from the truth and one turns him back, let him know that he who turns a sinner from the error of his way will save his soul from death, and will cover a multitude of sins" *(Jas. 5:19-20)*. By considering both our sins of commission and omission, we have a one-two-punch to fight the good fight against sin. Talking about it with our brothers and sisters around the Table translates into the well-being of the body, to which all are inseparably and wholly knit.

Holding down one's place in line, and exercising one's gift accordingly for the sake of the well-being of the entire body, is a vital part of any believer's responsibility to Christ's kingdom here on earth. We can cause the body to rejoice, or we can cause her to suffer. We can cause her to gather, or we can cause her to scatter. Communion can remind us regularly of our absolute obligation to fulfill our unique role when it comes to placement in the overall function of the body-corporate.

I believe Paul is telling us that when we fail to correctly observe the total spirit of Communion, we sin against Christ's personal sacrifice *and* the body-corporate as well. When we do that, we sin against the Great Commandment, which is to love our neighbors by being proactive

The Lost Supper

participants in the body's rejoicing, rather than dead-weights that lead to her suffering.

A Return to the Exodus

There are many comparisons we can make between the Passover of the Exodus, and the Communion ceremony of today. One of the most fascinating corollaries concerns this issue of our function within the soma, and how that affects her well-being. When the Death Angel went through Egypt, anyone caught outside the Passover ceremony would die, be he Egyptian or Israelite. If he was improperly partaking of the ceremony by being out on the street, rather than eating with the fellowship under the cross of the Passover Lamb's blood on the doorposts and lintels, he would pay an eternal price.

When Paul warns us of the judgment God will bring for unworthy participation in our modern observances, the message is, "Don't get caught outside the walls of this hallowed event. You call Him, 'Lord, Lord,'" even though you are disobedient to His Great Commandment to love others. Therefore, use this gift to repent and return to Him. Heed this warning and live or suffer dire consequences, as those left outside the fellowship in Egypt did."

There was something else that brought the Death Angel into camp that day. What was the sin so grievous in God's eyes that He was willing to take such extreme measures to get the attention of not only the Egyptians, but of His people as well? He said to Moses, "You shall say to Pharaoh, 'Thus says the Lord: Israel is My son, My first-born.' So I said to you, 'Let My son go, that he may serve Me.' But you have refused to let him go. 'Behold, I will kill your son—your first-born'" *(Exod. 4:22-23)*. The grievous sin of the Egyptians was their refusal to release the people of God to worship Him, through a journey of obedience that He had predestined them to take to the Promised Land.

As with all sin, we need to look past the action to the motivation to understand it. James tells us that we are tempted when we are caught up in our own lust. Then, when lust has found a good foothold, it gives birth to sin. Then,

> **Sin doesn't just happen. It is the outward manifestation of inward motivations.**

when sin is matures and grows into a lifestyle, it brings forth death

(Jas. 1:14-15). Sin doesn't just happen. It is the outward manifestation of inward motivations. How would we define the inward motivation of Pharaoh's sin? What was his attitude that made him so stubbornly resist the pleas of Moses for the release of his people?

In Exodus 7, we find the answer: "Pharaoh's heart was hardened, and he did not listen to them as the Lord had said. Then the Lord said to Moses, 'Pharaoh's heart is stubborn. He refuses to let the people go.'" Pharaoh's motivation for holding back the people of God was a heart that had become hardened—a heart that ignored the persistent, apparent, and overwhelming call of God, and stubbornly refused to give in to His divine will.

Fast forward to believers today, who persistently refuse the overwhelming evidence in the scriptures for a God who calls us all to mature in our faith through loving one another proactively. What could we say about those who refuse to contribute their gifts to the body, because they're too busy and preoccupied with seeing to their own needs? This is precisely the same type of stubbornness Pharaoh suffered from that invariably leads to a hard heart.

As we look at the amazing parallels between the circumstances that led to the destruction of the first-born of Egypt, and the weakness, sickness, and sleep [*death*] Paul witnessed in Corinth among the body-corporate, what do we see? What happens today when members of the soma live lives of disobedience, thus denying it the function of those specific members with which it would be stronger and more able? *They refuse to release God's people to go and worship Him through a journey of obedience that He had predestined for them—a journey that would lead them to the Promised Land if they would but go.*

Matthew Henry, writer of numerous commentaries on the Bible, says of the hard-hearted:

> Religious exercises are not acceptable to God if they are performed when we are in wrath, envy, malice, and uncharitableness. [Such] are sins so displeasing to God that nothing pleases Him which comes from a heart wherein they are predominant.... They who continue in a state of enmity to God are continually exposed to the

arrests of His justice, and the most dreadful instances of His wrath. 23

Just as Pharaoh held back the people of God from their kingdom-journey because of a hard heart, so those in the body of Christ who refuse to acknowledge their duty to edify her with their gifts, because of their hard hearts, hold *it* back. The penalty for Pharaoh and his first born was death. According to Paul in 1st Corinthians 11, the penalty for them today can be the same! God's body-corporate, the *soma*, will be hindered from proceeding on her path to the Promised Land carrying the burden of immature babes who refuse to leave behind those *elemental* teachings of Christianity, discover their gifts, and then deploy them in the interest of pressing on to maturity.

I believe the message here is a firm warning from the One who is watching over His bride, locked and loaded to do whatever it takes to see her through to the promised land of maturity. The message? *"Examine yourself. See what you are doing to My soma, My church, My bride. Judge whether you help or harm her. Discern whether you assist her in her voyage, or hold her back. If your contribution is lacking while you see only to your needs, wake up! Use this opportunity to discern whether or not you bury your talents in the ground. Don't harden your heart as Pharaoh did, by refusing to deal with your sin and accepting your place in My plan. Beware, for weakness, sickness, and death is standing at the door."*

Whether my thoughts concerning this issue are right or not, as important as the health of His body is to God, how could it hurt to ask ourselves [as a part of our self-exam at the Lord's Table] how we individually impact it? If the answer to this question proves troubling, the self-examination

> Communion is about more than where the individual discerns his or her standing with God. It is where the individual must confront where he is, or is not, with the collective.

process that God has granted through Communion is precisely where to get back on track. God designed His Table to be *the* forum for His children to seek answers to their questions, and pursue change through loving fellowship and Holy-Spirit conviction. Oh, the perfection of this!

Michael Wolff

Communion is about more than just discovering where the individual discerns his or her standing with God. It provides a holistic environment, where the individual discovers where he or she is within the collective of the church as well!

Jesus calls us to participate regularly with our spiritual families around the Table, where we can be naturally drawn back into our place in the fellowship. We can then become a blessing rather than a hindrance, and a source of her strength rather than part of her weakness. He gathers us, convicts us, and provides all of the tools to make us of one mind and one spirit, pressing on together to the Promised Land on earth He is forever calling us to.

IX: THE MATTHEW 5 ALTERNATIVE

How many times have we attended Communion services where hundreds, or even thousands, are present, and *everyone* partakes of the Elements? Think about it: when was the last time you observed anyone who called themselves Christian abstaining from the Elements? I have to wonder when I see men, women, and children—old and young in every stage of spiritual maturity, along with those I know not to be Christians at all—partaking so flippantly of such a holy ceremony.

Has everyone heeded Paul's instruction to examine themselves, and none found their heart or actions out of sorts with God's plans for them? How could this be among so many *sinners*? Are there no secret addictions, no closet love affairs, no un-confessed sin, and no harbored rebellion? No hard hearts? While our focus certainly shouldn't be upon judging others during Communion services, it is terribly difficult ignore when no one at all in such large groups abstains.

Given the current sad state of addictions in the church that poll after poll tell us exist, it seems unlikely that everyone in our large ceremonies could have passed their self-exams. It was evident to Paul that many in the Church at Corinth had failed, and yet wanted to partake anyway. Are we that much holier? Are we that much better? Or are we just deceived like they were? Are we just naïve, believing we are rich and in need of nothing when Jesus sees a far different picture?

If at this point you sense in your spirit that perhaps you have been partaking of the body and blood of the Lord irreverently, what are you to do the next time you come to His Table? If the Spirit is telling you that you are failing to contribute to the body with your gifts, or He has revealed a cover-up—if you have a love to embrace or an admonishment to consider, or your brother has something against you, and you have gone before the altar as an un-repentant prodigal guilty of stealing the fatted calf, what then? Will you ever be fit to partake again? If you are to consider abstinence, to what end? Is there biblical instruction as to what to do when you are in His presence, with the uneasy feeling that you have unfinished kingdom business to attend to?

Absolutely! In the power of abstinence we can find God's path to the ultimate victory in this fight-to-the-death struggle against self-deception. There is hope for you: that *way of escape (1 Cor. 10:13)* God promised. It comes in the form of what I call *The Matthew 5 Alternative*. The following story of a troubled young woman, and her release from a horrible prison of the past, will tell you why there is hope for all of us at His Table of truth and grace.

Julie attended her first Communion with us after attending our fellowship for approximately three months. She was introduced to us by one of the guys in the group who was casually dating her. He had had no more success at warming up to her than many others who had tried, for Julie was a very attractive, intelligent young woman. Her reputation, however, was of a girl who was friendly and fun to be with, but with an impenetrable shell blocking access to anything remotely below the surface.

We went up into the mountains above Denver on a warm summer night to enjoy Communion around a campfire. The more I taught concerning the importance of opening to the conviction of the Spirit, the more anxious she became. She flitted from small group to small group during time set aside for confession without saying much. Finally, as we prepared to take the Elements, she stood up and started pacing frantically back and forth. It was obvious to all of us that there was heavy-duty business going on between her and the Lord.

When we passed the Elements and completed the service, she abstained in obedience to the admonishments of 1st Corinthians. I prayed silently for her during that time, as I'm sure many of those gathered did. We all wanted to see her confess whatever it was that was gnawing at her spirit, so we could minister to her. Yet, we all knew the timing had to be God's, and so we waited.

A few minutes later, as we prepared to break camp and head back to town, she came up to me and said, "There is something I need to get off my chest. I know I will never be able to take Communion again until I do." This fifteen-year-old then confessed that she had been sexually molested by her babysitter when she was three years old. For twelve years she had never told anyone [save her mother at the time], who had dismissed it as a childhood fantasy. Now it all flowed out.

Hallelujah! Holy pressure! The Communion arrow had hit its mark! Twelve years of living with the pain and torment of this buried tragedy was released in one blessed night! All the guilt of thinking it was her fault, and all the fear of men lodged deep within her soul—fear that had kept her aloof and distant, was now exposed to God's glorious light! The evil one's plans to destroy her life were uncovered and exposed in one biblical Communion experience. And this happened to one who had participated in many Communion ceremonies over the years: powerless rituals that had left her a slave to her memories.

But there was a reason Julie knew she could find the strength to step forward. She knew there was hope. Because of something else we had discussed, she knew there was a way out of her prison. This story bears witness to a vital element of the Communion experience that allows for full conviction, and yet at the same time gives the offender hope. The Matthew 5 Alternative provides as way for those unworthy *now* to leave the Table without guilt, and with a plan that will give them with hope for victory in the *future*.

Remembering *There*

If we take Paul's warnings seriously, it is vital that we understand there is an alternative to either dangerous participation or abstinence without a purpose. That alternative is to abstain *now* from the Elements, yet with the goal of hope for the *future* in mind. Many who might otherwise consider abstinence look at it as defeat, or something to be embarrassed about, and so go forward and partake unworthily. Abstinence with a specific purpose in mind, on the other hand, is anything *but* defeat. It is rather a solution to the dilemma that comes upon us when our self-exam proves troubling, and our business with God is unresolved. Abstinence with the promise of hope is found in a short passage in Matthew 5:

> If therefore you are presenting your offering at the altar, and there remember that your brother has something against you, leave your offering there before the altar

Michael Wolff

and go your way. First be reconciled to your brother, and then come and present your offering.

In the opening sentence of this passage Matthew says, "If you are presenting your offering at the altar and *there* remember..." Why would this person *remember there* that someone had something against him? It is obvious that at some point he had harmed his brother. It is also obvious that he had rationalized and covered up his transgression. God knows this sort of thing happens all the time with His sinful sons and daughters. Therefore, He provided a time and place to deal with it. Once one understands the purpose and mission of Communion, the answer to "Why there?"

> He has us *there* remember because *there* is the specific place that He gave us to remember!

becomes clear. He has us *there* remember because *there* is the specific place that He gave us to remember!

If we will but honor the reason for the Table, humbly and earnestly seeking His soul-surgery, He will bless it by bringing to mind the very things He wants us to confront. If we will go to the Altar with the proper perspective on why we are there, He *will* honor it with a response. Only then can we begin the work of destroying the cover-ups, and all of their collateral damages.

What He will uncover are the sin-nature roadblocks we have allowed to remain hidden in our lives. They are the barriers that keep us from enjoying the fullest benefits available through our relationship with Jesus. They are also the ones that, left unattended, lead us in to emotional and spiritual undoing. If we will but let Him, He will *here* at the Table reveal these roadblocks. It is no mere coincidence that this passage begins with this truth. There is supernatural, divine power that opens to anyone who will endeavor to take advantage of it at His Table of truth and grace.

The Critical Question

We can use The Matthew 5 Alternative to resolve another, even more important question. As important as it is to set things right with our brother, I believe there is a larger issue here. In Luke 12, Jesus warns us as to whom we should ultimately ask the question, "Do You have something against me?"

> And I say to you My friends, "Do not be afraid of those who kill the body, and after that have no more that they can do. I will warn you whom to fear: fear the One who after He has killed has authority to cast into hell. Yes, I tell you, fear Him" *(Luke 12:5)*!

Will we one day all have to appear before the Judgment Seat of our brother? Will every knee bow to our brother? Will our brother have the authority to cast both body and soul into hell? There is only One who is worthy of such reverence, and only One who has this authority. That *One* is revealed as the Lion of Judah: Jesus *(Rev. 5:5)*. Jesus, the Lamb of God and Judge of men needs to also be asked the question, "Do You, my Lord, have something against me?" The One who knows my ways, thoughts, and very heart better than I myself do, needs to be consulted.

Typically following the commendations of Jesus to His Revelation churches for the good they had done, we find this message: "But this I have against you." This admonition is then followed up with warnings of dire consequences for failure to listen and repent. Our God is unquestionably a God of grace, love, and mercy—ever-ready to forgive and heal. Nevertheless, He is also a God of justice, and full of righteous fervor. He is a God of severity when dispensing consequence, as well as a God abundant when dispensing mercy. Jesus is a Savior and Judge to be both loved and feared—One that indeed will *have something against us* if we are fail to practice what we preach. The question, "My God and King, do you have something against me?" should be front and center during the Communion self-examination. Whether it be sin against our brother or our God the Spirit brings to our memory, what then?

The Healing Goal of Abstinence

If the answer from God to this question is "Yes," then the second half of The Matthew 5 Alternative is what gives us a plan, and hope for a brighter tomorrow:

> Leave your offering there before the altar and go your way. First be reconciled to your brother, and then come and present your offering.

At His Table, God urges us to go and take care of business with *dispatch* before we go on to focus on anything else in life. He knows that a little leaven affects the whole lump, and that we must be free of unconfessed sin to live as He intended—as *Freedmen*. In Proverbs 6, there is a parallel passage that also stresses this urgency: "If you have been snared with the words of your mouth, and have been caught with the words of your mouth, do this then, my son and deliver yourself. Since you have come into the hand of your neighbor go and humble yourself, and importune your neighbor. Do not give sleep to your eyes, nor slumber to your eyelids. Deliver yourself like a gazelle from the hunter's hand." Oswald Chambers, when teaching on these very verses, says:

> [Jesus] is saying, in essence, "Don't say another word to Me. First be obedient by making things right." The teachings of Jesus hit us where we live. We cannot stand as impostors before Him for even a second... When Jesus drives something home to you through His Word, don't try to evade it. If you do, you will become a religious impostor...Even at the risk of being thought of as fanatical, you must obey what God tells you. 24

We could compare true repentance to taking a driver's test, where there are both written and practical exams. Those who fail either part are expected to go back, review their studies, practice their techniques, and come back to get it right. Would you want incompetent drivers who failed their exams, yet were given licenses anyway, careening around causing accidents on your street? How about your surgeon or your airline pilot?

In Matthew 5, we are warned against presenting our offering while we know we have a test yet to pass. We are told to leave our offering there, go and answer the questions we missed, work on the technique we failed in, and come back to present our offering with renewed knowledge and experience. If God's Spirit quickens your spirit to *here remember* that there is work yet to be done, wouldn't it be wise to study, practice, and come back to get it right? Is it sufficient to pass the theoretical part of the exam [confession] without passing the practical exam as well [going and making amends]?

When we fail tests, we always have three options: 1) go back, better prepare, and retest, 2) quit, or, 3) proceed illegally. Far too few in the faith are taking advantage of the first option during the Communion test, and it's because far too few administrators are teaching the importance of it. Even when the warnings of 1st Corinthians are reviewed, without the Matthew 5 Alternative being proposed the suffering brother or sister is left with only two very unattractive choices: 1) they can choose what would amount to the illegal route in our analogy above by participating unworthily, which will result in them incurring God's just judgment, or, 2) they can choose what would amount to quitting in our analogy and leave feeling they are unworthy altogether to participate—now or perhaps ever again.

> **Without the Matthew 5 Alternative being proposed, the suffering brother or sister is left with only two very unattractive choices.**

Such people would either walk away without a proper fear of God, or without a proper appreciation of His grace. Regardless of their choice, they would go on in life in a self-deceived state, when Communion was ordained to shatter self-deception. By choosing option 1, The Matthew 5 Alternative gives participants instructions for dealing with their sin, a plan as to how to go about it, and hope for a victorious return once they do.

How many unstudied, unpracticed babes do we have careening around causing accidents in their lives and our fellowships? How many in the church could be counted spiritually weak, sick, and asleep? This circumstance could change drastically through a proper understanding of abstinence with the goal of reconciliation and victorious return. The Matthew 5 Alternative is anything but defeat! When you fail a test, and later go back, retake it, and pass, you more easily forget all about the failure. You begin to focus upon the newfound horizons that have opened to you as a result.

If you don't, however, all that is left to you is the sickening taste of failure. Then you have only two options: to accept defeat, or deceive yourself into thinking you weren't defeated, and go forward as a hypocrite. To avail ourselves of The Matthew 5 Alternative is to avail ourselves of the opportunity to, as Paul said, put the past fully behind us and press on towards the goal of the upward calling God has waiting for us *(Phil. 3:13)*.

I had a friend named Jerry in a men's group I once led. Jerry was one of those quiet giants who rarely said much, but when he did his comments were always thoughtful, wise, and well-reasoned. Every time Jerry opened his mouth it was "E.F. Hutton time." Everyone would stop and listen carefully to what he had to say. While we were both present at a Communion service one Sunday, Jerry and I were quietly discussing the issue of abstinence when he uttered one of those patented statements that made me sit up and take notice. He said, "Mike, the bottom line is that if your love of your sin exceeds your love for God, you'd better watch what you are doing here."

When Jesus confronted Peter after His resurrection, He demanded the answer to one question three times from this one who had forsaken Him thrice: "Peter, do you love Me…more than these" *(John 21:15)*? At the Table Jesus asks a similar question to all who have betrayed Him [which includes all of us at times]: "Child, do you love Me more than your sin?" The man who loves his sin more than He loves God will prove it every time he comes before the Lord's Table, and his treatment of the Matthew 5 Alternative will reveal both his heart and his choice. He will ignore the remembrances God gives there, refuse to truly participate in the process of repentance, and go forth to judgment. On the other hand, if we love God more than our sin we will refuse to be thieves of His fatted calf. We will be willing to do all necessary to go back, re-study, re-practice, and re-take the exam to win!

Why Not Let the Cup Pass?

To partake or abstain is the only litmus test Communion affords. To partake now, or leave our offering at His altar for now to return later in victory, are truly the only righteous choices we have. To participate or not *is* the qualifier, and the ultimate answer after our Spirit-led self-examination reveals to us where we stand with Jesus. To come before the Altar without thoughtfully considering the decision to partake or abstain is like trying to finish a course without taking the final exam. Under such circumstances, how can we possibly consider what we have learned or failed to learn? The worst possible disservice we can do to a struggling brother or sister, is to allow them to partake of the Elements while remaining slaves to a lifestyle of practiced and un-reconciled sin.

Matthew Henry speaks to our absolute obligation to consider carefully our participation in the blessed Table of Christ's ultimate sacrifice:

> From all this it is here inferred that we ought carefully to preserve Christian love and peace with our brethren, and that if at any time a breach happens we should labor for a reconciliation by confessing our fault, humbling ourselves to our brother, begging his pardon, and making restitution...and that we should do this quickly... Because, till this be done, we are utterly unfit for Communion with God in holy ordinances. [25]

...and Berkhof:

> From these words it appears that the Lord's Supper was not instituted for all men indiscriminately, nor even for all those who have a place in the church of Christ, but only for those who earnestly repent of their sins...and are desirous to increase in their faith, and to grow in true holiness of life. The participants... must be repentant sinners...And finally, they must have a holy desire for spiritual growth and for ever increasing conformity to the image of Christ...Even true believers may not partake of the Lord's Supper under all conditions and in every frame of mind...When a person is conscious of being estranged from the Lord or from his brethren, he has no proper place at a table which speaks of Communion. [26]

Many in the modern church think it a sin, or an affront to grace to let the cup pass. NO! *A thousand times, NO!* The only sin and unacceptable way—the only affront to grace at the Lord's Table, is to blindly partake when we are unfit. The focus should be self-examination in the interest of getting

> **Many in the modern church think it a sin or an affront to grace to let the cup pass. NO! *A thousand times, NO!* It is no sin to let the cup pass.**

real with God, rather than participating in the Elements for appearance's sake. The people outside the walls of our churches, along with an increasing number inside them, are losing patience with a religious system that seems to exist only for appearance's sake.

Believers know God's plan is good, but somewhere along the line, manifesting the Gospel in real life isn't working. Their connection with the practices of the faith have become compromised, yet they can't seem to put their finger on just why. One of the reasons these same people pass by the doors of churches on their way to 12-step programs or therapist's chairs, is due to the reality check they get there that is missing in the church. One of the reasons these 12-step programs work is the simple fact that they unwittingly employ the Matthew 5 Alternative:

> We made a list of all persons we had harmed, and became willing to make amends to them all…We made direct amends to such people wherever possible, except when to do so would injure them or others. [27]

Believers caught up in sinful behaviors would see the same sort of power to heal, and more, if we returned to the precepts of biblical Communion the 12-steps and therapists practice. As unbelievers and believers alike now flock to these programs for healing and restoring reality to life, so they would flock back to the church if we offered them the same tools.

It is no sin to let the cup pass while you go with haste to be reconciled with your brother, or your God. We need to accept the challenges the Holy Spirit presents per the first part of Matthew 5, and then act obediently upon them per the second part. This is an opportunity granted us in Scripture like none other—an opportunity to break out of the grip of superficiality, and into the reality of the life abundant with Christ! But that will mean a paradigm shift in our understanding of abstinence. We need to stop perceiving it as guilt and defeat for the sinner, but rather to view it as hope for victory over the sin.

The beauty of The Matthew 5 Alternative is this: it doesn't leave us forever *estranged* from the Communion Table. It invites us to use it to mature, and accept the challenges of discipleship. It keeps the lines of healthy conviction and unhealthy guilt drawn clearly in our minds. One of Kimbrough's devotionals reveals the following contrast between guilt and conviction:

> There is guilt. And then there is conviction. Guilt depresses, defeats, demoralizes. Conviction motivates and redirects. Guilt is a seed planted strategically by the devil that crops up at the most unexpected times to remind us of how pathetic we are. Conviction is an uncommon gift from the Holy Spirit that may come wrapped in sandpaper and burn all the way down. But its purpose is to redeem, to restore, to renew [author unknown]. 28

The Lost Supper is the place to embrace conviction, thereby exorcising the guilt that has built up from refusing to face it. It can, and usually does, *burn all the way down*. Yet, to go on day after day in ignorance is even worse. The guilt that comes from ignoring sin will eventually depress, defeat, and demoralize anyone. The burning lasts but a moment, but the depression can last a lifetime. When we ignore God's genuine tools for dealing with sin, we automatically grab hold of the counterfeits. When we reject the real deal of conviction, we *always* and *automatically* embrace the counterfeit of guilt.

I admire those who abstain now and then [with a goal of purity] because I know, as painful as an inside look can be, they have taken their sanctification seriously. They have gained a clearer understanding of the spirit of Communion, their God, and themselves. Many times I have had to let the cup pass myself, because I realized something was amiss—times when I have felt the conviction in my spirit that I had unfinished business to attend to. I trust fully in the grace I have seen Jesus grant me *seventy times seven*, but because of the knowledge that I have refused the promptings of the Spirit in some area of life, I know partaking would only lead to superficiality. I have refused to be trained by His discipline, and know that I lack the peaceful fruit of righteousness that comes from it.

Those who have learned the power of abstinence make tremendous progress toward becoming real with God. Rather than insulting grace, they have shown a profound appreciation of being bought with the price of that grace. They have understood, and been faithful to God through honoring the purpose of His Communion. Such people will never again entertain the kind of superficiality that results from prolonged periods of self-deception.

God has a different message for each of us, depending upon where we are in our walks with Him. What is important is whether we hear what He is saying and act upon it, rather than whether we partake or not. If done for the right reasons, and in the proper spirit, abstinence and participation are one in the same. Both are acts of obedience, and both are an indication of the functional moving of the Spirit in our lives. Abstinence should never be looked upon as failure to participate. The true failure exists in unworthy participation, and *only* there. Again, I refer to Matthew Henry's warnings:

> **If done in the proper spirit, abstinence and participation are one in the same. Both are acts of obedience.**

> To be exact and severe on ourselves and our own conduct is the most proper way in the world not to fall under the just severity of our heavenly Father... O! let all look to it that they do not come together at any time to God's worship, and all the while provoke Him, and bring down vengeance on themselves. 29

Abstinence no Crutch

A final thought before we leave this subject: The Matthew 5 Alternative isn't about punishment, or making sinners feel unworthy. However, it could be if used as a crutch rather than a call to action. Abstinence should only be for a short season, hopefully not past the next observance of Communion. This is where the fellowship of the spiritual family comes in. When a sin is confessed that leads a participant to abstain, it becomes absolutely incumbent upon the rest of the fellowship who received that confession to see to it that the amends are made, the work is done, and that person returns the next time in victory.

Bearing one another's burdens is a command to the fellowship of true disciples. It is the one and only *law of Christ*. Allowing one to abstain over the same circumstance for an extended period of time is not the intent of Communion, nor of The Matthew 5 Alternative. Don't let this become a punishment in the eyes of the one abstaining, or a crutch that allows practiced sin to continue on un-reconciled. Come alongside your brother or sister who has seen fit to abstain, be a part of their next ceremony being a victorious one, and fulfill the law of Christ.

Again, please understand the way God set up this wonderful system to work. The repetitive nature of Communion makes it an ideal setting for consistent, continual maintenance of the believer's emotional and spiritual state. If you sense the conviction something needs to be done, or change needs to be made that you have been fighting, abstain, take real steps to bring yourself back into God's will, and then return the next time to partake. This is the victory! This is good! This is the way it was designed to work. The Communion self-examination isn't about conviction for conviction's sake, but about encouraging true repentance that brings about necessary action—and that leads to transformation and victory!

When we take honest, painful steps towards becoming real with God, and bringing about the changes He seeks, it is anything but failure. It is the victory! Employ The Matthew 5 Alternative every time you come to the Lord's Table. Its message will give you both instruction as to how to deal with the Spirit's convictions, and hope for a brighter tomorrow when you can return and present your offering in confidence—having received an A+ on your self-exam.

X. THE BEST CONFESSION

> Therefore, when I admonish you to confession I am admonishing you to be a Christian. 30

> We admitted to God, to ourselves, and to another human being the exact nature of our wrongs 31

I have come to have grave concerns regarding the particular brand of confidentiality we have embraced in the church. One of the many falsehoods secular psychology has brought within our walls in the guise of Christian therapy is a dangerously *exaggerated* sense of the need for confidentiality. It has given all of the fallen Sons of Adam and Daughters of Eve a new place in the Garden of Delusion to hide out. The need for confidentiality has now become the standard excuse to continue cover-ups for many who, in truth, would rather go on in denial of their closet carnality than deal with it. Within her hollowed halls God's people, who don't want to confront their sin and yet still feel good about themselves, have found the perfect escape.

Why is it that when most small fellowship groups gather together and ask for prayer requests, most of our brothers and sisters will only let us in to the shallowest of the deep dark secrets that lay within the recesses of their souls? "Nothing wrong here. I'm doing okay," they say with practiced smiles firmly posted to hide the pain. Then they will typically defer their request to anyone they can think of who struggles with some terrible disease or circumstance.

Are they genuinely concerned, or are they trying desperately to get the focus off of themselves? What are we to believe, when the very next day they will go pay a therapist they barely know an excessive hourly wage to spill their guts? Why have Christian counselors become the church's new superstars? Why is it therapists have eclipsed even pastors concerning the respect their advice commands? Why have counselors become the accepted path to healing in the church, while most fellowships struggle with intimacy and depth?

While there are certainly times when we must consider who to confess to under certain circumstances, God never intended our sin to be *confidential*. Sin lives, thrives, and finds its perfect growth culture in darkness. It is repulsed by the introduction of the light of the Spirit, truth, and fellowship into the equation. One reason there is so much practiced sin believers struggle with today is the darkness of denial in which their sin is allowed to perpetuate. Self-deceived believers can sit through endless sermons talking about all aspects of repentance, and remain totally unfazed unless they decide to become proactive about it. It usually takes much more than a good sermon and rousing worship to crack the shells of the cover-ups. Bonhoeffer says to this:

> Sin demands to have a man by himself. It withdraws him from the community. The more isolated a person is, the more destructive will be the power of sin over him, and the more deeply he becomes involved in it, the more disastrous is his isolation. Sin wants to remain unknown. It shuns the light…In confession the light of the gospel breaks into the darkness and seclusion of the heart. The sin must be brought into the light. The unexpressed must be openly spoken and acknowledged.32

If we bring in the holy light that only confession to God *and* man accomplishes, darkness simply cannot survive. However, exposing sin to light never comes easily. The trick is to put those deceived by unreconciled sin into an environment where they will dare to face it, and that is just what God has provided for them at His Altar. Would God encourage us to examine ourselves, and then abandon us once we had honored that command? By no means! But we need to take full advantage of this precious gift, lean upon the body to help us confront our transgressions, and then press on in faith that He will truly give us everything we need to live lives that reflect godliness *(2 Pet. 1:3)*.

Jesus never intended our confessions to be handled by ethically detached people, forbidden by the worldly licenses [the ones they share with secular psychologists] to love us. Jesus confronted people anywhere and everywhere, in public and in front of whoever was present. He came to expose sin to the light and deal with it, and never allowed the targets of His rebukes the luxury of the sort of confidentiality that has become the norm in the modern church.

It would have been against His very nature to pull Peter aside and whisper to him, "Get thee behind me, Satan," in the interest of confidentiality. Did He rebuke His disciples privately when they could not cast out demons, or find enough food to feed the five thousand? Did He pull Judas aside privately at the Passover when He revealed him as the betrayer? Did he confront the Pharisees in confidentiality when He called them a brood of vipers, or clear the temple discretely of its moneychangers?

Did Paul, in the name of confidentiality, quietly pull Peter aside to admonish him concerning his hypocrisy with the Jews? No, he got in Peter's face in front of everyone *(Gal. 2:14)*. How was it that the believers in Christ's Pentecostal church of Acts 2 were all together daily, and had *all things in common*, if confidentiality is what they were seeking? Communion is the way God seeks us out in our hiding places, urges us to confess to a that multitude of counselors Solomon says will bring us victory *(Prov. 11:14, 24:6)*, and makes us stop hiding behind what we call confidentiality. To confess among our brothers and sisters in the body who are commanded by godly license [not forbidden by worldly license as are the Christian therapists], to love us and pray for us, bring accountability, and walk closely with us through to the end—is a far better solution. However, the fellowship can only help us if they know what's going on.

I believe one of the most powerful aspects of the 12-step programs is addicts simply gathering with others afflicted with their own problems, and finding a solution. Each one confesses their struggles to, and are supported and held accountable by, the others in the group. There are no therapists needed within these programs, just sinners willing to be obedient to biblical mandates of confession within the fellowship. How sad the church has failed to understand what they have understood.

Healing is accomplished where two or more sinners who can say, "Been there – done that" get together in God's name for confession, prayer, a call to action, and the support and love to carry it through. Simple confession and prayer between two brothers or sisters is the way to healing according to James 5:16.

> **All that is required for healing is two or more sinners willing to be obedient to the biblical process of confession within the fellowship.**

No degrees necessary, just two or more gathered who have been tempted themselves, that they might come to the aid of others who are also being tempted *(Heb. 2:18)*. It is the way Jesus did it.

Each one of us has experienced the thorn-in-the-flesh kind of sin we struggle with daily, and yet often times seem powerless to do anything about. When we give in consistently to these sort of temptations, we begin to play myriad forms of mind games to try to explain to ourselves how it is we fail to beat them. We begin to justify, rationalize, or just deny our problems, and do a slow fade into the darkness of lawlessness.

Those trapped in this state of numbness to their sin usually lose sight of two very important truths: 1) they have power abundant to deal with their sin, because God has given them all they need to fight, and, 2) He is still ready, willing, and able to forgive them, and let them begin anew with a clean slate. Neither of these mean they will necessarily be freed from their desires, for Paul sought freedom from his thorn in the flesh and God said it was better for him to struggle with it. But it does mean that there will always be hope, and that God will not allow us to be tempted beyond what we can endure.

The Good, the Better, and the Best

When I was a young boy at Christmastime, I used to love to thumb through the large department store catalogues. One in particular grouped the gifts into *good, better, and best* categories. Of course, my eyes would immediately wander to the "best" category first. Then I would always look at the other two, to see what it was that was "best" about the best. I would compare price and quality to see what it was that made the others inferior [and, of course, to formulate my intelligent arguments forthcoming with my parents as to why I had to have the best]. As I began to reflect on the concept of self-examination that Paul tells us is so critical to a rich and healing Communion experience, those old Christmas catalogues came to mind.

I asked myself, "What is the best way to self-examination?" Is confessing to God alone the best way? Well, that may be good, but is it the best? Do I confess to man alone? Well, that is certainly good as well, but is it the best? I came to the unalterable conclusion that if I wanted to avail myself of every weapon God had given me to fight this fight—if I wanted to pull out all the stops to take a truly in-depth look at the monster dwelling in my flesh—then confession both before God *and* man would be the best way to go.

> If I wanted to pull out all the stops, then confession both before God *and* man was the best way there was.

The admonishment in 1st Corinthians 11 says that a man is to examine *himself*, rather than, "But God will examine the man." While the Spirit's critical eye is certainly extremely important, and it will be He who will guide us through the process, this is also an exam God wants us to engage in through an act of our own will. Therefore, we play a part in doing the most thorough and best examination possible. Few ever undertake the truly frightening step to seek God's conviction. They do feel it when it is impressed upon them, but don't proactively seek it out. This is why God gave us this forum to give us a proper place to engage.

The problem for the self-deceived heart is even worse. It no longer feels conviction even when God is knocking. Lawless people *practice* a particular sin pattern, while at the same time ignoring the Spirit's calls for repentance. They become numb to all forms of conviction. An attack from both God and man is required at this conjuncture to strip away the façade, and open up their souls again to the Spirit's promptings. It takes the *best* sort of confessional process to root out the very worst sort of cover-ups.

It is for this reason we don't take the Passover alone, but are told to do it within the confines of intimate spiritual family. If it was just about seeking forgiveness in private prayer—the only opportunity typically given to us in most modern ceremonies—why not just do it alone with Him? If the only necessary element of our self-exam was to pray to God, why gather? Matthew 6 would tell us the best way would be to do it in the secret of our closets if it was all about prayer. Yet, our clear model of Communion is brothers and sisters gathered intimately together, to help one another through the process.

The very nature of self-deception demands that her victims see no need to fight. If one understood why one was deceived, one by definition would *not* be deceived! Being deceived precludes us from seeing clearly, and thinking rationally. By definition then, we are *only* deceived when we are and we think we aren't. This makes it impossible to break out of our condition alone, because we have crossed the line of clear thinking concerning our condition. We fail to see the warning signs, and thus continue on hopelessly adrift in a cozy blanket of spiritual dysfunction. How, then, can we even pray earnestly for forgiveness, having lost any conviction for transgressions now fully denied? God's persistent calls have been ignored, so a few private moments to pray to a God we've disconnected our true experience from won't do any good at all. Here the reality of where we stand with Christ remains lost in a bizarre twilight zone. Bonhoeffer explains:

> By sheer grace, God will not permit us to live even for a brief period in a dream world...God is not the God of emotions, but the God of truth. Only that fellowship which faces such disillusionment with all its unhappy and ugly aspects, begins to be what it should be in God's sight, begins to grasp in faith the promise given to it...A community which cannot bear and cannot survive such a crisis, which insists upon keeping its illusion when it should be shattered, permanently loses in that moment the promise of... community. Sooner or later it will collapse. 33

When people become self-deceived, they create roadblocks between themselves and God that close channels of communication. Isaiah says of this:

> Behold, the Lord's hand is not so short that it cannot save, neither is His ear so dull that it cannot hear. But your iniquities have made a separation between you and your God, and your sins have hidden His face from you so that He does not hear.

Why does He not hear?

> For our transgressions are multiplied before Thee, and our sins testify against us...conceiving in and uttering from the heart lying words. Justice is turned back, and righteousness stands far away, for truth has stumbled in the street, and uprightness cannot enter. *(Isa. 59:14)*

God's hand is easily long enough to reach, and God's ear is easily keen enough to hear. Rather our iniquities, if *multiplied* long enough and not repented of, create the separation between us. When we live in this condition of lawlessness, our transgressions stay with us. We deny the Lord, and turn away from His piercing convictions. We speak lying words to ourselves from deceived hearts, and justice is turned back. Righteousness stands far away, and God's just command and right thinking remain distant. Those who think Jesus came to die to forgive the unrepentant of the sins of a deceived and lying heart need to meditate on these words for a while. This kind of denial puts even the child of God on the thinnest of ice, and it takes another human being with the words of God in his mouth to come along and create a crisis in his life to shatter it.

Proactive confrontation *is* about creating this crisis in the life of the dreamer and the self-deceived. Without the help of the multitude of counselors God has placed in the body, the self-deceived person remains hopelessly adrift in a sea of superficiality—double-minded and unstable in all their ways. They don't get better. In fact, Paul tells us they will only get worse. He says that evil men will proceed from bad to worse, and that they will go out *deceiving and being deceived (2 Tim.*

> **Proactive confrontation is about creating a crisis in the life of the dreamer and the self-deceived.**

3:13). Those with hard hearts deceive others with their hypocrisy, and deceive themselves in the process. Satan, in concert with their own pride, has blinded them to the truth. He has put them to sleep to their condition. It is therefore sin for the disciple to refuse to confront self-deception in their brothers, and by doing so leave them adrift and hopelessly confused. It is a violation of both the Great Commandment to love them, and Christ's law to bear their burdens.

The truth is we all need help to avoid the rationalization of the sin which so easily entangles us, and slowly leads us down the slippery slope to self-deceived superficiality. To those who have lost grasp of the reality of their condition, and the truth of how to be freed from it, Communion can be a vital lifeline. When we couple God's remedy for attending to our emotional and spiritual problems [fellowship], with an atmosphere of confession, prayer, and self-examination [Communion], we arrive at the *best* biblical recipe for dealing with self-deception, both for the victim and the counselor.

However, when we don't provide the opportunity because we water down the Communion message as we have, the self-deceived person can go on hiding. He can slink off into the darkness of silent confessions that over the years have lost any faith in the power of a seemingly far-away God. But such people can't hide from the one-two punch of God's conviction, and their brother's intervention in an intimate spiritual family setting. I defer to Bonhoeffer once more:

> Where Christians live together the time must inevitably come when in some crisis one person will have to declare God's Word and will to another. It is inconceivable that the things that are of the utmost importance to each individual should not be spoken by one to the other. It is unchristian consciously to deprive another of the one decisive service we can render to him. 34

Jesus constantly declared God's words and will to others, as a service to them. One of the great tragedies of the modern church is we have stopped speaking the truth to one another about the true character of Christ, the nature and consequence of sin, and the will of God. In our ever-increasing attempts to make the church a more comfortable, non-threatening environment—and Jesus a nice, non-threatening person to be around—we avoid confronting one another at all costs.

Jesus never compromised His character or His message for anyone: sinner or saint. The Rich Young Ruler *(Luke 18)*, the Samaritans *(John 4, Matt 15)*, the Pharisees *(Matt 23)*, the politicians *(Mark 15)*, and His own disciples on occasions too numerous to mention found this out the hard way. Many who said they desired to follow Him were turned away because they wanted to follow some Jesus that conflicted with the genuine article.

The need for leadership that will show the same integrity with the character and the message of Jesus that He showed for Himself has never been greater in the church. The need for righteous judgment within the fellowship has never been greater in the church. Yet, the number of those willing to speak the truth to sin-addicts has never been fewer. As Bonhoeffer said, "It is unchristian. " The lack of righteous judgment among believers has led us to the most *unchristian* church in American history.

Why Darkness Lives

There are at least three reasons I have found that people fail to enter in to the power of speaking the truth to one another about the character and message of Jesus Christ, thus allowing sin to flourish in darkness while superficiality thrives. First, we seem to have a lack of mature shepherds endowed with the knowledge of the Word, and the spiritual backbone to confront those entrusted to their care. We're so concerned about them being offended—so consumed with concern that they will leave us to find another fellowship.

That seems strange, given the fact that the counseling business is reaping record profits because believers are looking for a firm hand to help them deal with their struggles. As we have increasingly turned the job over to them, we have suffered a corresponding loss of authority held by church leadership. Jesus confronted everyone with the truth—including His disciples—and it lead people to marvel, "This One speaks as one in authority, not as our leaders in the Temple" *(Mark 1:22)*.

Leaders of God's often wandering sheep have an absolute *mandate* to be righteously judgmental, in the interest of fulfilling their duty to protect the purity of the body. Paul warned the arrogant leadership of

The Lost Supper

the church at Corinth that they were kidding themselves if they thought he was unaware of their deceptions, and acting as though he would condone their conduct. He warned that he would indeed go to them, and soon, if God willed it. At that time he would refuse to listen to their words, but would get to the heart of the matter.

He then asked them how they would like his rebuke served up: with a baseball bat, or in a spirit of gentleness? He didn't hesitate to confront their self-delusions and arrogance, and reminded them he didn't need to be present bodily to have already *judged* the offense *(1 Cor. 5:3).*, Here Paul reveals the heart of a true shepherd, as he boldly confronts unconfessed, festering sin. His message? "Deal with this yourselves, or you'll be hearing from me and my Louisville Slugger*!"

There is only one way to renew repentance to a hard heart that continually ignores biblical calls to repentance, and that is go as far as is necessary with church discipline to deliver the shock treatment required. When a heart has stopped beating, it's time to take out the paddles and turn up the voltage, which includes removal from the fellowship if necessary. Paul was so assured of his position, and so confident in the power and discernment he had been given by God that judging righteously and without regret came naturally. How sad the leadership he addressed was remiss in displaying the same confidence and understanding of their position, power, and responsibilities to act with righteous judgment. What a pity so many of our church leaders today find themselves mired in the same malaise, when it comes to fulfilling their mandate for righteous and loving judgment of those placed in their care.

> **Mature leaders have an absolute mandate to be righteously judgmental when it comes to sin in the body.**

And as hard as it is for leadership, it is even more difficult for one layperson to extend a word of admonishment to another. Bonhoeffer observes:

> What a difficult thing it often is to utter the name of Jesus Christ in the presence even of a brother! Here, too, it is difficult to distinguish between right and wrong. Who dares to force himself upon his neighbor? Who is

> entitled to accost and confront his neighbor and talk to
> him about ultimate matters? 35

Too often we let awareness of our own shortcomings keep us from acting upon what we know is the right thing to do for the good of another. We must remember that God does not ask us to be perfect before confronting our brother, rather He has made the body such that where one brother stumbles, another has been fashioned strongly *(1 Cor. 12)*. While we all harbor sin, we are also all given strength in certain areas. We don't all struggle with lying. Some are strong concerning addictions to drugs and alcohol. Others have been given strength in the area of lust. Rather than being ashamed of our sin in one area, let us press on to strengthen our brothers where they are weak and we are strong.

God has fashioned us, and placed us all in the body to serve one another. We hold others up in our strength, that they may hold us up in our weakness. That process will never see the light of day if we don't have the guts to step to the plate and take a swing at superficiality in the life of our brother, knowing full-well that we are all sinners. The desperate need we feel for the grace of God over the vileness of our own state, should serve to urge us on to help our brother in the mitigation of his. That we ourselves are sinners should in no way keep us from our duty to our brother, unless we are guilty of un-confessed sin that has rendered *us* hypocrites.

If we have heeded the command of Jesus to get the log out of our own eye, by being repentant ourselves, we can go help our brother *(Luke 6:41)*. If it were sin that kept us from speaking the truth in love, would we have any preachers of the Word? Any teachers? Any ministers at all? The man who denied Christ three times in His hour of need says, "But sanctify Christ as Lord in your hearts, *always* being ready to make a defense to everyone who asks you to give an account for the hope that is in you" *(1 Pet. 3:15)*. Jesus later told Peter that once he had recovered, he was to *go and strengthen his brothers*! What a perfect picture of the grace of God working through sinners like us! It matters not what kind of day we've had, or how weak or hurting we may find ourselves under the weight of our own struggles. Nothing, absolutely nothing, must keep the true disciple from righteously confronting his brother in his hour of need.

Lastly, darkness is allowed to live through the misguided notion that, once Christ has initially climbed into the gutter of sin in our lives to save us, He expects perfection. He wants nothing more to do with our dirt. This is the One who sought out harlots and criminals. This Jesus returned to those who fled from Him in His hour of need, and gave them the keys to the kingdom of heaven. When the Father formed His first children, He formed us from the dust of the ground. When Jesus healed the eyes of the blind, He spit upon the ground and made mud to use as a balm. Would this One who got His hands dirty first to make us, and then again to restore our sight, stop getting them dirty to sanctify and consecrate us as we walk with Him through life?

> **Does it occur to us that Jesus was most effective was when He was made least attractive?**

Does it occur to us that Jesus was *most* effective was when He was made *least* attractive? He was soiled most by our sin on the Cross of Calvary, and He did His best and most lasting work there! Jesus longs to get His fingers dirty in our lives, if it means our sanctification and spiritual growth. He lived daily with his band of twelve sinners, confronting their problems with both a rod and a spirit of gentleness, as He built a fellowship that would have to endure tremendous persecution upon His leaving. He longs to bring His light into our dark closets, if it means they will no longer hold putrid rags of practiced sin. Once again, Mr. Wells:

> As a believer, it is easy to turn one problem into five. You fall out with God before you fall into [sin]. Fall into condemnation and your problems will multiply. You must learn to get up as fast as you fall. Condemnation drives you from Him, where you will be sunk and move into angry rebellion. 36

I would say that the next step beyond angry rebellion is the numbness of lawlessness, when the sinner is no longer able to acknowledge his sinful practices because he has denied and rationalized them for so long he feels Jesus either remains ignorant to, or gives hearty acceptance to, his sin. Many times it starts when we believe He couldn't forgive us again—for that same old sin *again*?

Oh, how Jesus longs to forgive us—again—for that old thorn in our flesh as we approach Him with new humility, repentance, endurance, and willingness to get up as fast as we can and get back into the race! He may not remove it if He decides it is preferable to our pride getting out of control *(2 Cor. 12:7-9)*, but He will always forgive it. But He will only come in and soil His hands if we invite Him through a belief in His willingness to forgive us as many times as we do. He still stands at the door and knocks upon our sinful, fleshly lives, but He won't kick the door open.

If Jesus told Peter to forgive his brother seventy times seven, how many times will He forgive us, wash us whiter than snow, and give us a brand new start? If we'll but return to Him with repentant hearts, and empty hands, how many times? He was the One who said, "Greater love hath no man than this: that a man lay down His life for a friend" *(John 15:13)*. He's in it for the long haul. He's in it for the gutters as well as the mountaintops.

Communion's self-examinations can free the self-deceived, if those administering it will display courageous leadership, get past their own sin through personal repentance, and trust in the Jesus that still delights in soiling His hands to clean us up. When placed in an environment where proactive self-exams and confession are properly nurtured, the light bulb of realization can be switched back on for those in denial, and too intimidated or enmeshed in the cover-up to break out before.

When the process of self-examination through confession to God *and* man is made a required and normal element of the ceremony, everyone involved will find it easier to accept help, because everyone involved will partake themselves. They won't feel the need to present a false spiritual face, when participating in a process where all are involved in confrontation and confession. In the properly understood and administrated Communion setting, they will see little need to hold up such facades. As Bonhoeffer asserts, neighbors accosting and confronting one another when it comes to ultimate matters will be the rule.

Proactive confession through proactively seeking the Spirit's conviction, along with the confrontational fellowship of other believers, is truly the *best* method God gave us to complete a thorough self-exam, because every weapon in God's arsenal is employed to root out any deeply entrenched sin-addictions. If there were more true confession going on between brothers and sisters in Christ, we would see a profound reduction in the instances of spiritual sickness in our churches, and put most of our therapists out of business.

I close with Dr. Crabb, the man who wrote the book on Christian therapy but now has found a better way to be a catalyst of God's healing within the fellowship of believers:

> We no longer struggle together with our deepest concerns and our most internal battles…We rarely share in a way that requires the Gospel for the community to survive and for meaningful bonding to occur. The masks remain in place, we tell only of our stories, we deal [a bit proudly] with emotion-laden struggles that don't disturb our final commitment to independence, and we find ways to connect that don't require the depths of…grace. 37

If we offered more opportunities for brothers and sisters to gather in settings conducive for struggling with our deepest concerns, and our most internal battles, there would be far more reality and depth in our relationships, and far more healing of emotions in the church. These settings can be facilitated through the Lord's Table if we move past merely good, or better, and on to sharing in a way that requires the meaningful bonding of the Christian community to occur.

The goal of the Communion confessional is to find ways to connect that require the deepest depths of integrity, reality, and grace. This was the goal of the writer of Acts, as he exclaimed, "In view of this, I also do my best to maintain always a blameless conscience both before God *and* before men" *(Acts 24:16)*. A blameless conscience is a healthy conscience. A healthy conscience equals a healthy emotional state.

XI. PRAYER AND CONFESSION: THE PROCESS

> Many argue that forgiveness is unconditional, but those two words do not go together for "unconditional" implies that there is no sin. And if no sin, there can be no forgiveness. Yet, all have sinned, and through confession "He is faithful to forgive us our sins"…Forgiveness and confession are two words that are inseparable, and should remain together. 38

The practical application of the self-examination process comes forth primarily through two activities. While I have alluded to these philosophically, their practical application within the Communion environment, make the Table the two-edged sword God intended. Accomplished within a setting of confrontational love, sincerity of heart, and humility, surgical prayer and loving confrontation make all the difference in a fruitful Communion ceremony. All worship and teaching has been to prepare souls for this moment, as the group must now come together to see to it that no one [save unbelievers, who again are encouraged to stay and observe] fail this crucible so crucial to fruitful self-examinations, and thus emotional health.

Participants must now unite as a body, because the truth from God can, and most often does, hurt. It is a necessary hurt, a glorious hurt, a healing hurt, and a sanctifying hurt—but *hurt* nonetheless. When we are hurting, we need others in the body acting as a body by bearing our burdens to help us get through it. We also need to know the healing of forgiveness, and contrary to popular opinion in the church today, forgiveness and confession are two words that are inseparable. There are two directions in which we must focus confession, to make the self-examination both thorough and effective. Both are ways that God has ordained to shatter the curses of superficiality and hard-heartedness in men:

The Lost Supper

Vertical Confession

> We sought, through prayer and meditation, to improve our conscious contact with God…praying only for knowledge of His will for us and the power to carry that out…We made a list of all persons we had harmed, and became willing to make amends to them all. 39

The first confession we must engage in is *vertical*, coming humbly before the throne of God to proactively seek His conviction of sin through individual prayer. Paul says, "But the One who examines me is the Lord. Therefore do not go on passing judgment before the time, but wait until the Lord comes, who will both bring to light the things hidden in the darkness, and disclose the motives of men's hearts" *(1 Cor. 4:5)*. God is the only One who can truly begin our self-exam. For the fellowship to attempt it before God reveals the conviction *is* passing judgment—possibly erroneous judgment—before the proper time. Once Jesus has passed judgment on the sin itself, the fellowship can begin to judge itself and act according to His will.

> **There is no amount of human interaction that can open up one's heart to the conviction of sin, apart from the Holy Spirit's leading.**

There is no amount of human interaction that can open up one's heart to the conviction of sin, apart from the Holy Spirit's leading. Therefore, the best way to prepare for a time of group confession is to get alone with the One who knows us better than we do, and ask Him to illumine the things hidden in the darkness, and make known to us the motivations of our hearts. It is through this time of proactively seeking God's conviction, that we *here remember* those hidden motivations. The Holy Spirit will bring these remembrances to all who will but seek Him right now, right here, at the place He especially ordained for it.

The group should be broken up so that everyone, individually, can quietly find a place to be alone with God. In the quiet of their time, all should be encouraged to reflect upon passages such as the 1ˢᵗ Corinthians verse above, Philippians 4:6-7, 1 John 1:9, and Psalms 139:23-24, before they begin to pray. Make copies of the Prayer Recorder [available at the end of this chapter] and hand them out to everyone before they go to prayer. These verses are included, along with areas to record what God may be saying to them for their own benefit, or for the benefit of others.

This again is why 12-step programs have attained an effectiveness we rarely experience in the church today: they follow the biblical mandate to pray with a purpose of cleansing the soul. If I might reverse the order of steps 8 and 11, the message here is to seek to improve our conscious contact with God, pray for knowledge of His will for us, and the power to *carry that will out* in real life. We must be as the house built upon the rock—as people who hear the Word of God's conviction, and then act decisively *(Matt. 7)*.

This prayer time is not a time for intercession for others, or worship. The believer walking in superficiality has—and will continue if allowed—to use such prayers to avoid the necessary surgery into their heretofore hidden sin closets. This is a time to confess known sin, but more importantly a time to listen intently to what the Holy Spirit has to say concerning sin hidden for too long in the darkness of a hard heart, or ignored in the numbness of rationalization. We are seeking here only for knowledge of His will, and the power to carry that out, and nothing else. Once that connection to God's Spirit has been made, participants can use the Prayer Recorder to make a list of all persons [including God] He reveals who may have something against them.

There are two benefits that prayer to God offers the sinner that can be found nowhere else:

- ✦ The conviction of sin that reaches deeply into our souls, and causes confession *and* deeds in accordance with repentance. If we will but ask, God will reveal to us everything we need to understand about our sin, and what we need to do to deal with it. He will bring to our remembrance all admonishments He wants us to consider, and also the love He wants us to embrace, as He did with His disciples at His Passover.

    We all fear the consequences of this kind of invitation to the truth, but it's such a silly anxiousness in light of the fact that Jesus already knows every dark thought, and every dark deed we have had or done. We are merely inviting Him to show us that which He already longs to reveal. Journaling any thoughts that come to mind during this time on the Prayer Recorder will help everyone to focus on what's truly important, and will provide a future personal prayer and action list for each participant.

> We are merely inviting Jesus to show us that which He has already been longing to reveal.

✦ The forgiveness and grace that God alone grants: confession of sin before God is where we seek forgiveness through the blood of Christ. Proverbs 1:5 and 28:13 tell us that forgiveness comes through vertical confession. Jeremiah says of this, "I will not look upon you in anger, for I am gracious,' declares the Lord. 'I will not be angry forever. Only acknowledge your iniquity, and that you have sinned against the Lord'" *(Jer. 3:25)*.

Most people readily understand and accept this, although I do find that many—myself too often included—have trouble grasping its power. It is very difficult to believe in God's forgiveness sometimes, particularly when we deal with those *thorns in the flesh* that torment us daily. Is it His lack of effectiveness, or ability to forgive sin, that keeps us under clouds of guilt? Or is it our own lack of faith in that ability? As participants enter in to this time of confession, encourage them to open up and hold nothing back. Each conviction that remains unattended to keeps us that much further from the healing Jesus desires we accomplish here. This is the ordained time to let all the ugliness that is within come out, and to offer up heartfelt pleas to our gracious God for His mercy that waits in abundance! Encourage renewed belief and trust in that body broken and blood of the New Covenant of grace and mercy poured out, as all wrestle with a God who delights in the struggle.

Encourage participants to at least *begin* opening up their heretofore hidden closets of practiced sin patterns. While for many it will be hard, at least initially, to take on everything they know they need to bring to light, they must at a minimum be willing to start working on that list they will [hopefully] be writing down on the Prayer Recorder. To fail to do this is to give that which is causing weakness, sickness, and sleep a continued stronghold. There will be future opportunities to continue the process at later observances, so don't try to force it. However, the confession process needs to, at the very least, be initiated or the participant must be warned to abstain. Refusal to engage at all indicates repentance feigned, and superficiality reinforced rather than shaken. That shuts the door on emotional healing and God's mercy, and opens the door to His promised and proper judgment.

Finally, during prayer each person should be encouraged to seek more than just the *knowledge of His will*, but also for the *power to carry it out* during the confessional time to come. Prayer without the follow through in confession and action will be revelation without result, and only serve to deepen the deception. For every cover-up revealed, God will also grant the power and strength to confess and act.

Revelation of sin during prayer time is just the beginning of a process designed to fully restore, renew, and heal. The Grantor of that revelation wants us to press on, and carry it through to the very end! Through years of phony tearful confessions by substance abusers, 12-step administrators have come to realize that, without following the process all the way through, little fruit is yielded. So don't let the confused stop with vertical prayer and horizontal confession alone. Encourage prayers for both the understanding of the Spirit's convictions, *and* the power to carry true repentance—in both word and deed—out to the Lord's desired conclusion.

Horizontal Confession

> We admitted to God, to ourselves, and to another human being the *exact* nature of our wrongs. [emphasis mine] 40

Once called back from prayer, the discussion can begin for the second step—the one that this Passover setting was tailor-made for, yet one rarely observed in the modern church. This is the one that is the difference between merely attending Communion, and genuinely experiencing that fellowship that exceeds mere association awaiting us there. This is the one that can complete the breaking process, and bring about profound healing and change to those who will have the faith and courage to embrace it. It is confession before the brethren: step five of the 12-step, and the critical ingredient to make the experience all that God intends. It is admitting to another human being the *exact* nature of our struggles. Examining oneself—one of the two prime directives of the ceremony according to Paul—cannot be experienced fully or effectively without it.

This isn't to be a time for vague confession concerning what sinners we all are, but rather to take the Prayer Recorder and confess the *exact* nature of our own personal struggles with sin to another human being. Generalizations here might soften the blow for the moment, but they only continue the prolonged suffering. The time of small-group confession is also a time for those hearing confessions to write down any burdens they feel they should bear for those confessing. This may be a commitment to pray for someone, intervene in a dispute, hold someone accountable to a Communion commitment, or to just come quietly alongside someone in their hour of need.

It is important to record these things, because issues revealed during prayer time are ones that were important enough to the person, and to God, that He had them *there remember* whatever they are. Confession exists as much for the good of the confessee, as for the confessor. It is an incredible opportunity missed to bond the fellowship in love, if commitments made to follow up are ignored by either party.

There is a passage that defines true biblical healing, and within it a verse unique in all of scripture that sets mutual confession apart as so absolutely critical to the healing of the soul. Unlike numerous passages that deal with God's forgiveness through confession to Him, James 5:13-20 takes a unique perspective in how the involvement of the fellowship brings *healing*:

Is anyone among you suffering? Let him pray *(Jas. 5:13)*.

We all come to the Communion Table suffering under the burdens of sin, for human beings—even redeemed ones—sin daily. This is why we need to pray during the ceremony specifically over those issues that have brought about our suffering.

> Is anyone among you sick? Let him call for the elders of the church, and let them pray over him *(Jas. 5:14)*.

It is critical that once a confession is made in the small groups, others receiving that confession pray on-the-spot for the one doing the confessing. Matthew tells us that whenever two or more gather together, God will be in their midst *(Matt. 18:20)*. Healing through biblical fellowship hinges upon two or more coming into agreement in the presence of God.

> And the prayer offered in faith will restore the one who is sick, and the Lord will raise him up. And if he has committed sins, they will be forgiven him *(Jas. 5:15)*.

Again, this is all part of a glorious process that, if followed through to its conclusion *will* work! It begins with the sick person realizing the source of the illness, and calling for help from the fellowship. Once that is done, it becomes incumbent upon the fellowship to do their part. When it all comes together, as it was divinely inspired to do within the environs of the Communion experience, it does work. The sick are restored to holiness in the sight of God, and forgiven—period. But there is one final step yet to be taken that will lead to true healing:

> Therefore, confess your sins to *one another* and pray for *one another* so that you may be healed. The effective prayer of a righteous man can accomplish much *(Jas. 5:16)*.

This is the message we must understand while gathered around the Table of Healing, and the one our well-intentioned therapists have missed altogether. This is the final step of the process that brings true restoration that we now go looking for in all the wrong places. The pure logistics and psychology of large groups gathered where little time or effort is expended on the process, precludes effective confession during Communion services that now dominate the Christian landscape. Likewise, the clinical setting and doctor-patient relationship of therapy precludes one to one healing James 5 intends. The Passover was administered house-to-house and mano-a-mano, and not attempted in the Temple or the doctor's office—either by Jesus or His Pentecostal Church.

This is the vital, life-giving part of Communion that establishes intimacy, builds rooted and effective small-group fellowships, and will bring about results that will amaze you. There is no hiding here. There is nowhere to run. When confession, one to another, is employed after earnestly seeking God's conviction within the perfect environment for self-examination, the floodgates of the living water of Christ burst forth in a kaleidoscope of emotion, relief, self-revelation, and cleansing of the soul! This is true for those confessing, for those forgiving them, and for those who respond by fulfilling their responsibilities to fulfill Christ's one and only law. And, finally:

> My brethren, if any among you strays from the truth and one turns him back, let him know that he who turns a sinner from the error of his way will save his soul from death, and will cover a multitude of sins *(Jas. 5:19-20)*.

It *all* works for *everyone* involved when we honor the Lord's Table, by entering into human confession of sin. Both sinner and restorer find healing and forgiveness when this divinely ordained process is fully engaged in by Jesus' children, at the specific place He gave for engagement.

To summarize the effectiveness of this passage, the truths found in James 5:

- ✦ Force us to humble ourselves: This is a vital process in the life of the growing disciple. We can many times remain hardened in our hearts, all the while praying dutiful [but often meaningless or hopeless] prayers to God. Such façades cannot be upheld when confessing sin face-to-face with a brother or sister in Christ. Pride of spirit disintegrates in the light of confession in the flesh.

- ✦ Bring sin out into the light: We as believers were created to deal with our sin before God, and within the fellowship. It is an innate sense of the need to confess that has caused many in the modern church to abandon shallow fellowships [where they are not able to confess] for the counterfeit of therapy [where they are]. Anyone who hasn't known the liberating, freeing experience of fully exposing their sin to the light of fellowship is living under a burden none of us was intended to bear.

The need for the fellowship of our brethren is a deeply rooted desire that God weaved into our souls, because we were built for relationship. People want the closeness that confession and intercession provide, and they will go wherever necessary to find it. This is why even sterile relationships with therapists are preferred by many to superficial and shallow relationships with those they call "friends."

There are too many living under the persistent guilt of un-confessed sin, and believers struggling with the consequences innately know that fellowship is the answer. Even though the process of confession may be painful, and perhaps humiliating, it is temporary, and is always followed by the peaceful fruit of righteousness for those who have the courage to engage. The yoke of remaining under the crushing burden of un-reconciled sin, however, is pain multiplied a thousand times over. It never stops, never sleeps, and never takes a holiday until God is honored through confrontational confession and prayer relationships within the fellowship of the saints.

> **The yoke of remaining under the crushing burden of un-reconciled sin is pain that never stops, never sleeps, and never takes a holiday.**

✦ Bring about accountability: Accountability can be left behind if prayer is the only avenue sought to healing. When our sin is in the open, our brothers and sisters can check up on our progress—a process that strengthens both parties to the confessional. This is what bearing one another's burdens is all about. We're not left to police ourselves concerning our commitments to deal with sin. Doing that, as the self-deceived do, is leaving the proverbial fox in charge of the henhouse. When you combine confession and prayer, though, you can achieve that blameless conscience before God and man. How can one have a blameless conscience before both, without confessing to both?

- Bring about true fellowship: Paul tells us that fellowship refreshes our spirit. In part, it is able to do that by helping us understand that we are not alone in our weaknesses [something Satan wants us to believe so we reject fellowship], and that we can have all things in common through our similar struggles and combined strength. Where secret lives of un-confessed sin exist, true fellowship is but a myth. This is why most small groups in the modern church fail to go deep enough to bring about healing.

    The culture of superficiality thrives where those who harbor such practices are allowed to think they are in fellowship, when in fact it is leaving them unfulfilled. They are allowed to be physically present, though in truth their hearts remain far from God, and far from others in the group. There is no deep or lasting experience of fellowship, or of grace, because there is no discipline or suffering that always brings about the passion and integrity required for the depth we all crave. Without confession of sin to one another, and prayer for one another, James 5 healing stands at a distance, as does the testimony to the power of fellowship that makes it so very desirable.

- Help us avoid future struggles: Confession to another helps heal past and present sin, and it is also many times the fear of having to answer to our peers aware of our struggles, that helps us fight the fight against developing future sin patterns. Many times knowing I must face those who know my sin [because I have confessed it to them], and confess *again,* is a great deterrent to giving in to temptation. It is not my faith in God, or my spiritual maturity, much as I would like to claim it. Rather, it is obedience to His system of confessional fellowship that I believe He blesses.

    Proper follow-up with those who have confessed their sins to one another will keep accountability as a vital part of small-group fellowships. It will forge lasting friendships, as members of the Communion will realize they have true brothers and sisters who will courageously invade their lives with truth in love, for their own good.

- ✦ Establish a valuable practice of experiencing and participating in brotherly love: Experiencing the Communion self-exam, and then participating in the follow-up, will make it easier at any time for the members of your fellowship to enter into true confession whenever they feel the hand of God's conviction. True brotherly love comes through all of these things, lived out and evident, within an environment of Christian fellowship. Words alone will never get us there, nor will superficial relationships without depth.

- ✦ Provide encouragement: Paul told the Romans that he longed to see them, in order that he might impart some spiritual gift to them because he desired to see them established in their faith. He wanted to be encouraged together with them, as he was among them in an interaction of mutually beneficial faiths *(Rom. 1:11)*. The writer of Hebrews urged the church to consider how to stimulate all to love and good deeds. He warned them not to forsake the assembling of themselves together, as some were doing. He wanted them to have a sense of urgency in their desire to encourage one another *(Heb. 10:27)*.

   How many times are we encouraged by the word of our brother or sister, when God's voice has been silent? How often are we lifted by just the presence of a kindred spirit in times of crisis or need, or encouraged by just observing the love others in the fellowship have toward one another? There is an edification and love that we can only receive through interaction with other human beings. God has ordained this, so that we would be His body on this earth. We won't find it in Him alone, because He won't allow it. If He did, would we seek out the fellowship of other believers? And without that, would we ever know true love? How would the world, then, come to know us by *our* love, for this is the way Jesus said true disciples would come to be known *(John 13:34-35)*?

James 5:16, Ecclesiastes 4:9-12, Hebrews 10:24-25, Matthew 18:15-20, and Proverbs 11:14 and 24:6 all admonish us to seek out the help of the fellowship in dealing with life's challenges. Bonhoeffer explains:

The Lost Supper

> We must ask ourselves if we have not often been deceiving ourselves with our confession of sin to God, whether we have not rather been confessing our sins to ourselves and also granting ourselves absolution. And is not the reason perhaps for our countless relapses and the feebleness of our Christian obedience to be found in precisely the fact that we are living on self-forgiveness and not real forgiveness? (This) can never lead to a breach with sin... Who can give us the certainty that, in the confession and forgiveness of our sins, we are not dealing with ourselves but with the living God? God gives us this certainty through our brother. Our brother breaks the circle of self deception. 41

...and from Rob Bell:

> It is one thing to be saved. To believe in Jesus. It is another thing to be healed. It is possible to be saved and miserable. It is possible to be saved and not be a healthy, whole, life-giving person. It is possible for the cross to have done something for a person, but not in them...I learned that salvation is for all of me. I learned that Jesus wants to heal my soul—now. And for Jesus to heal my soul, I had to stare my junk right in the face. 42

At the risk of being redundant, I cannot stress strongly enough the circle of self-deception that leads to superficiality and hypocrisy comes through the experience of extended times of unchallenged, practiced sin patterns. This involves perhaps years where prayers have been more self-absolving than real, and where fellowship has been shallow and non-confrontational, rather than effective. It leaves us feeling miserable, even while we know deep inside God has saved us.

> **I cannot stress strongly enough that the circle of self-deception that leads to superficiality and hypocrisy comes through the experience of extended times of unchallenged, practiced sin-patterns.**

Michael Wolff

Participatory Repentance

> We were entirely ready to have God remove all these defects of character...We made a list of all persons we had harmed, and became willing to make amends to them all...We made direct amends to such people wherever possible, except when to do so would injure them or others. 43

This is taking confession to the next level, why 12-step programs are more effective than anything the church is offering, and why people don't find the healing they could be through the gifts of Communion available to them. 12-step administrators understand the biblical way of repentance better than the church does, it seems. The kind of repentance we see in the above steps exposes and heals sin-addictions, where a few minutes of private, confidential prayers we allow in church ceremonies has failed so miserably. We have incorrectly been taught that knowing what to do is all that counts, yet actually putting it in to practice has become optional. Even the best confession will fall short if we fail to put feet on it, and show by our deeds as well as our words that we are ready to truly change.

In Rick Rusaw and Eric Swanson's *The Externally Focused Church*, a book every disciple of Jesus on planet Earth should read, the following is written about putting feet on our words:

> Good news and accompanying deeds are like two wings of an airplane...Each gives 'lift' to the other. To study the life and ministry of Jesus is to study a tapestry woven of good news and good deeds. Woven throughout the fabric of His life was a ministry of Show and Tell—of good works and good news, side by side, working powerfully together...The good deeds paved the road over which His good news traveled. 44

Much the same could be said about the actions of repentance. Repentance travels from word and tongue over the road paved with deeds, on its way to transformation of the sinner. Without deeds as a part of the equation, our multiplied words of repentance to God avail us little of holy sorrow's transforming power.

> **Repentance travels from word and tongue over the road paved with deeds, on its way to transformation of the sinner.**

As Paul made his defense before Agrippa in Rome, he described his duty to see that those who heard the Gospel understood the meaning of true repentance. He would do this, by declaring to anyone who would listen, that performing deeds of repentance was as important as saying words, and the two together proved humility was in the heart *(Acts 26:20)*. Repentance without deeds is a dead end road of endless apologies to God without life transformation. This is the whirlwind we have reaped today through an endless string of Communion ceremonies, with little true healing or change taking place in participant's lives.

Robert came to me during a Communion confessional. He said the Spirit had been constantly reminding him of an experience that, up to that night, seemed trite to him. He had damaged a fence with his car coming out of his high school parking lot four years earlier. Suddenly, after years of burying the memory, it was all he could *remember* that Communion night. I suggested to him it was obviously something God wanted him to deal with, and to be attentive to the Spirit's promptings. I believed Jesus was calling him to action.

Some days later, he called me and told me he had gone to the owner of the fence, asked his forgiveness, and said that he wanted to make restitution. The owner was so amazed at this young man's honesty [the fence had been knocked down many times by other students over the years, yet Robert had been the first to fess up] that he gathered his whole family in the living room to talk to him! Robert was presented an opportunity to share the Gospel with an entire family, all because he took advantage of proactive deeds of repentance.

In 2 Kings, chapters 22 and 23, there is a story about an amazing king and man of God. It is a story that magnificently illustrates the concept of participatory repentance, and its effect on an entire nation.

We are told Josiah did right in the sight of the Lord. While there were many good kings found in the books of the Kings, even the many who did some good things left out one critical act in the repentance process. They didn't tear down the high places where sacrifices were made to pagan gods. This angered God greatly, and He communicated as much to Josiah in response to his prayers. God said that His people had forsaken Him by burning incense to other gods, and that this had given Him wrath that would not be easily quenched.

So, unlike his predecessors, Josiah decided to act. As the story in verse 4 of chapter 23 plays out, he commands the high priest and his followers to bring all of the vessels that were set up for false gods out of the Temple, so he could burn them. He then did away with the false prophets and priests whom prior kings had appointed to burn incense in those high places. He then dealt with the astrologers who burned incense to constellations. He ground all of the idols in the temple to dust, and threw the dust on the graves of the common people. Josiah then removed all the sanctuaries on the high places which former kings of Israel had set up, that provoked the Lord. He slaughtered all the priests of the high places he could find on their own altars. He removed all of the idols, and their prophets, that were anywhere to be found in the land of Judah and Jerusalem.

These actions—this participatory repentance unlike any of the kings before him—caused the following to be written of Josiah:

> And before him there was no king like him who turned to the Lord with all his heart, and with all his soul, and with all his might according to all the law of Moses. Nor did any like him arise after him.

Think about it! This list that included King David and King Solomon, but among them there was *no* king who ever followed God like Josiah did? What is truly fascinating to note as a result of all of Josiah's repentance, however—and germane to our discussion—is what happened next:

> Then the king commanded all the people, saying, "Celebrate the Passover to the Lord your God as it is written in this book of the covenant." Surely such a

Passover had not been celebrated from the days of the
judges who judged Israel, nor in all the days of the kings
of Israel, and of the kings of Judah.

Did Josiah just come up with the idea to celebrate the Passover after this proactive repentance by himself? No, for at long last the stage had properly been set for the Passover due to repentance in deeds as well as in words! It was only then that God put in Josiah's heart to institute the Passover again. The Table had finally been properly prepared by a courageous shepherd, and a people who had turned their hearts and minds back to Him. Not even in the golden age of Israel, when David and Solomon reigned, had there been such a Passover celebrated!

This story shows us that we, too, can celebrate a Passover/Communion such as we have never celebrated before, where participatory repentance causes us to connect with our heavenly Father and our fellowship as never before. When sin has lost all its power, and is no longer able to tear the fellowship asunder, true communion between the sinner and the brethren, and the sinner and God, is restored in a glorious reunion made possible through this magnificent ceremony. Chambers says of such repentance:

> **Today we, too, can celebrate a Passover/Communion such as we have never celebrated before!**

> Beware of saying, "Oh, I am longing to be sanctified."
> No, you are not. Recognize your need, but stop longing
> and make it a matter of action. 45

How it Looks

How can this proactive repentance manifest itself in our modern ceremonies? Shoe-leather repentance can take on many forms, from the simple to the extremely delicate and complex. Simple or complex, it is never easy. There are times when we would do more harm than good to confront certain people who have been involved in our transgression. Without proper discernment and wisdom, we can dig up buried skeletons of a type that would cause others suffering, even as we made personal efforts to repent. This violates step 9 of the 12-step, the Great Commandment to love our neighbor, and the intent and spirit of Matthew 5. We need to make direct amends to such people wherever possible, except when to do so would injure them or others.

We must always consider the character of the sin, along with the spiritual maturity of people we need to approach, and ask if our confession hurt them, even as it heals us. If so, we should find someone who may know both parties involved, or may be aware of the situation, and confess it to them. That person could then do whatever the effective follow-up would mandate, without causing harm to another. The important thing is to get sin on the table, and expose it to the light of both God and the fellowship. We need to get beyond the mere longing to be cleansed and healed. We need to make repentance a matter of action.

Another obstacle can be one of pure logistics. Many times, we may find ourselves in the position during a Communion service where personal contact with those we need to mend fences with just isn't possible. While Matthew 5 makes it clear that we need to come to the altar *after* repairing damaged relationships with those who have something against us, I believe a sincere verbal and personal commitment is enough to allow one access to the Table. If the Communion Table is fenced properly, and an environment of reverence established, you won't need to impress upon the confessor the seriousness of his or her Communion commitment before God and the brethren [note: I do not mean making promises or "covenants" of any kind, for the Scriptures warn us against that. We need to simply let our yes be yes, and our no, no *(Jas. 5:12)*.]

Then there is the case where returning to fix a wrong is just impossible. While Matthew 5 is to be taken seriously, needlessly crucifying ourselves over past mistakes we cannot go back and right is fruitless. Always use discretion. Pray about whom you wish to confess to, what circumstances God wants you to deal with, and how. If you need help in understanding certain situations, remember always Solomon's admonition in the Proverbs: "Where there is no guidance, the people fall, but in abundance of counselors there is victory" *(Prov. 11:14)*. God will provide the right person for every confession, and discernment in each situation when we honor the ceremony by doing the best self-exam possible.

If the commitment to do whatever it takes to proactively follow through, and begin anew in a growing relationship with Christ—and that commitment is verbalized—then participation in the Elements should be encouraged. Part of the follow up of the fellowship is seeing to it that commitment is fulfilled before the next observance. The commitment on the part of one, becomes a commitment on the part of the fellowship, when Christian love becomes more than mere words. If a Communion commitment is verbalized, and then the confessor fails to act upon it, you need only to wait for the next ceremony to help them again confront the issue. However, this time they need to be instructed to abstain from the Elements until real action is taken, inasmuch as during the previous Communion a verbal commitment was made and ignored.

A perfect opportunity is provided here to help the self-deceived understand exactly how superficiality works, and how it might have found a place in their lives through false repentance. Superficiality always results when people think words are actions. People cannot escape their obligations to act upon their words when the repetitive nature of Communion won't allow it. That is precisely the practical, functional beauty of it all! This is the power of action-based repentance. It is also the philosophy behind the concept of sponsorship in the 12-step programs. Superficial commitments mouthed, and then ignored, only serve to heap sin upon sin, and deepen the delusion of self-deception.

> **A perfect opportunity is provided here to help the self-deceived understand exactly how superficiality works.**

Too Much of a Good Thing

I once heard a pastor discussing a meeting he had with a homosexual man, who wanted very much to be a part of his church. The pastor asked him two very astute questions that should be on the minds of all gathered when participating in the self-examination process. The first question the pastor asked him was, "Do you want God's will for your life?" The man responded, "Yes, I do." Then the pastor asked him a question that was a little bit harder to swallow: "Do you want God's will for your life—even if it's not what you thought it might be, and calls you to change what you may be thinking or doing?" The man hesitated, but then said, "Yes, even if that's what it means." The pastor smiled and said, "Welcome on board, then."

A willingness to come into God's will—even if it means changing the way we think or act—is what God seeks from us at the table of truth and grace. As with any good thing, too much can reverse the benefits and cause harm. Don't overdo it. This process of participatory repentance and confrontation will do more damage than good if taken to Pharisaical extremes. It isn't about ritualistic works, but rather establishing a humble practice of self-examination, leading to revelation and cleansing. Unrealistic mandates producing self-condemnation will turn a biblical opportunity into an unbiblical chore. Such practices will replace Christ's yoke that is light with man's yoke that is burdensome. With many who have never experienced true repentance, baby steps will many times be as fast as they can move.

The important thing is that they are moving on a path back to Christ, and away from cover-ups. We must encourage that one step into faith, rather than badgering someone for failing to conquer all of their demons at once. Practiced sin patterns are formed over extended periods of engagement, and demanding the road out be short and fast can crush spirits, destroy trust, and damage any good accomplished.

God won't let those participating be burdened beyond what they are able. We need to be a part of what *He* wants done, and knows *they* can handle. All need to just listen to His Spirit, and make efforts to act depending upon the urgency of His prompting. Just getting to the point of opening themselves to God's convicting power, and acknowledging denied or rationalized sin in general, will be a huge step in the right direction for many.

Pray for wisdom for all to know when to press, and when to back off. Pray for spiritual discernment among the flock, especially for your Communion shepherds. Pray for a spirit of tough love and compassion during this time, that will be evident to all. The idea is to provide those attending with an environment conducive to opening up as yet unrevealed or undealt-with areas of sin in their lives, and then acting on them. The Lost Supper is a place where the fellowship fulfills the law of Christ, by bearing on its broad shoulders the burdens people have been bearing alone.

Finally, leadership needs to stress at this point that if anyone will not confess, and be ready to act upon at least some of the issues God had them remember, *abstinence* is the only safe course. This is *not* legalistic, and those who administer the Table must stand strong against any claims it is. According to Matthew 5, everything God has caused them to *here remember* is for a reason. If the superficial or self-deceived are allowed to wriggle out of the confessional process of the Communion ceremony, superficiality will be allowed to go on unopposed.

> This is the place where the fellowship bears on its broad shoulders the burdens people have been trying to bear alone.

Beyond that, it *will be reinforced in the hearts and minds of the self-deceived,* which is in large part what has caused the cancer of weakness, sickness, and sleep we see so prevalently displayed in the body of Christ today. Communion was given to us to stop superficiality's deadly whirlpool of delusion. If it is allowed around this Table designed to dismantle it, it will be allowed to continue as an accepted way of life for the participant.

The buck of rationalized and denied sin stops here at the Communion Table, because here is where God said it was to stop. The superficiality born from practiced, un-confessed, covered-up, un-reconciled sin stops here! Communion is ordained to shatter walls of denial and phoniness, not enforce them. This is a part of the self-examination process that simply must be encountered head-on, and pressed through, regardless of any temporary discomfort. Be strong and of good courage. Stay the course, employ the rod God has given you in love, and shatter the deceptions!

Confession before God and man, that bears the fruit of a blameless conscience before both through real participation, gives 12-step programs and the ceremony they were founded upon their power to heal.

XII. ET TU, JUDAS?

And if your hand causes you to stumble, cut it off. It is better for you to enter life crippled, than having your two hands to go into...the unquenchable fire (Mark 9:43).

I believe Judas was a far more important player in the Passover scene than a quick review might indicate. There is a message we need to hear from his seemingly normal life as a disciple of Christ, and his tragic death and everlasting legacy as a betrayer of Christ. Both he and Pharaoh were unique players on the same stage, yet at different times in biblical history. They were both seemingly cursed from birth in ways we will never understand this side of heaven, and both likewise predestined to suffer damnation to accomplish God's two exoduses for His people. There is much to be learned from their mistakes within a discussion of Communion. Though Judas' part in the Passover play occupied little copy, its message to us is immense.

Jesus never merely taught. He *always* lived what He taught. Judas' dismissal was one of those teachable moments, and an example to us of how we need to treat the unrepentant participant at Christ's Table. God has placed each member in the body to edify it—to make it stronger and more capable. However, if there should be a Judas who causes stumbling, that member needs to be identified and subjected to church discipline [up to and including removal from the fellowship], rather than allowing the whole body to suffer.

One of Jesus' opening comments at His Passover meal was, "He who shares My bread has lifted up his heel against Me" *(John 13:18).* To lift up one's heel against another, means to injure them through employing *deceit*. When we partake unworthily in the Lord's Table, what do we do other than to lift up our heel against Jesus by [as Paul says] sinning against the body and blood of the Lord? As a result of Judas' own self-deception, his heart became closed to Jesus' influence, and opened to Satan's influence *(Luke 22:3)*. Once that happens, deceit is second nature.

As it was then, so it is today that when we come to the Table in rebellion we injure the soma-corporate through our deceit, and mock Christ's soma-personal through unworthy participation. Without examining ourselves, repenting, and acting, we become thieves of grace and open ourselves to numerous attacks of the master of deception. We transform the Table of freedom that exorcises Satan's influences from our lives, into the Table of judgment that invites him into our lives. By this act Paul would tell us that Judas' *weakness* was revealed, his *sickness* was exposed, and his eternal *sleep* was assured. Jesus was not about to give his disease any chance to spread to the rest of the body, by allowing it at His holy Table.

> **By this act Judas' *weakness* was revealed, his *sickness* was exposed, and his eternal *sleep* was assured.**

The Spirit who searches our hearts and minds knows exactly where we are when we come to Communion. As in all things, Jesus gives us freedom of choice. If we have allowed the light in us to become darkness *(Matt. 6:23)*, and we stiffen our necks to His persistent calls to repentance, then He will allow us to seal our fate. Only Jesus knows what's truly going on within us, and while administrators of the Table can look for signs of hard-heartedness, and admonish those who would partake unworthily, Jesus alone is the final judge and executioner of consequence.

If the self-deceived are determined to lift up their heels against Him, even after proper teaching and time allowed for confession, He will allow it, as He allowed Judas to partake of the Elements to seal his fate that evening. He will allow us to bring judgment upon ourselves, rather than violate His own laws of free will that He gives to those He desires to love Him.

Judas' story reveals the practical application of properly fencing the Table. Jesus allows Judas his free will to partake, but also confronts his deception. When Judas will not repent, and is intent upon carrying out his ungodly plan, Jesus abandons him to his deceptions and dismisses him *with dispatch*. There is no place for people like Judas whatsoever at a Table that speaks of Christ's sacrifice, for their perversions have turned the light in them into a darkness that they refuse to sway from—a darkness that will spread to the body if we allow it.

But can we say with certainty that Judas was an unbeliever, and simply dismiss his part in this? Is it possible for us to be modern-day Judases when we come before the Lord's Table? I think that Judas was a believer, although confused and influenced heavily by a group known as the Zealots [Barabbas' misled clan]. This was a group that hated the Romans with a passion, and viewed Israel as a kingdom-in-waiting, ready to return to prominence after the Romans were evicted. They believed in civil unrest, and inciting violence among the Jews to fight the tyranny of Rome. The Zealot's image of the Messiah was of a warrior-king, leading the Jews to a glorious liberation of Israel. Jesus came performing miracles, and speaking with the authority of the Messiah, yet He rejected the role of king in favor of humble carpenter, itinerant preacher, and servant of all. He was therefore rejected by this sect, who were looking for a warrior.

I believe Judas' thinking on that Passover night could have gone something like this: "I know what I have seen Jesus do. He's turned water into wine, fed thousands with a few fish and loaves of bread, raised the dead, and calmed stormy seas. I know that He is the Messiah, for who could else could do such miracles? I also know that many in power in Israel are, like me, looking for the Messiah. They preach about it, they pray about it, and they tell us to constantly keep watch. I think there is just a great misunderstanding here. If I can only get the parties to meet face to face, and the temple leaders would come to see Jesus as I see Him—if Jesus will just understand that if He combines His influence with those now in human authority, we can rise up and take back our land. We can become the Israel of old again!" But Judas was dead wrong.

Judas not Unlike Us

While he did eventually betray Jesus, it is clear that until the day this whole nasty scene in Jerusalem unfolded, Judas wasn't unlike any of the other disciples. Like all of them, he followed Jesus daily. He went out to minister in His name when told to, he sat at His feet to learn, and endured Jesus' unnerving rebukes just like the others. Without Judas' betrayal, would any of us read the Gospel's accounts of his actions, and think of him any differently than the other eleven? We could make a good argument that the intent of Judas to force this meeting was not for the sake of seeing Christ's ministry on earth terminated, but rather expanded.

And isn't it ironic that his act of betrayal did just that? Not that I wish to glorify Judas in any way, but even though he used all the wrong methods, and harbored all the wrong motives, his act of betrayal led to the explosion of Christ's ministry through His death, and the coming of the Holy Spirit. Where once one man indwelt with the Spirit did the work of the ministry, there were now twelve that would soon become thousands!

If Judas were an unbeliever, and his mission in life was to see Jesus' ministry derailed, why then his comment to the temple leaders when he tried to return the coins which had purchased Jesus' death? Why such remorse as he cried, "I have betrayed innocent blood?" Wouldn't he rather celebrate as he realized the success of his plan of betrayal, if killing the Messiah was his intention? Unless he believed in Jesus, why would Judas hang himself in despair as he came to understand, in one hideous moment, he had secured his legacy as history's most infamous traitor?

No, I think Judas was a believer—one not so different from many who claim to believe in Jesus today. This is why it is vitally important to understand the role of Judas in the Passover. How did he get to this unenviable place? Notwithstanding his unique position in history, how did he come to be so confused and vulnerable to deception?

At some point during his life, Judas came to believe in Jesus enough to leave all he had and follow Him, for that was Jesus' unbending standard for His disciples. Through all of his travels with Jesus, do we think that Judas had a goal to have his name recorded in infamy? Did he harbor thoughts of growing up history's most reviled figure as he watched Jesus perform miracles, teach, and love people? Do we think for a moment that Judas preplanned all of this, looking forward to the day when he would hang himself in remorse, and be constrained to hell's torments through all eternity? Really?

Up until the point of his treachery, wasn't Judas is like many of us who have all the right intentions as we go through life? Didn't he, like us, want good and wonderful things to happen to ourselves and others as a result of our influence? We all want to go out of this life satisfied that we left a legacy of serving both God and our fellow man. Then somehow we get off course. It always begins when we make one wrong and seemingly insignificant choice. If we don't deal with it, however, that one small wrong leads to another [many times to cover up the first one], and another, and another. Our small and seemingly insignificant wrong snowballs into a very significant change in the way we think and act. We find ourselves looking back at those glorious plans we had as youngsters, wondering where it all went so wrong.

> Judas is like many of us who have all the right intentions as we go through life… But then somehow we get off course.

How many young boys dream of dragons to slay, and tales of heroism and adventure to leave in their wake, only to end up in dead-end jobs and loveless marriages? How many have their lives dictated to them by needs to pay the mortgage, build a retirement nest-egg, and put the kids through college? How many of them grow old, look back on lives of drab existence and wonder how they could have wasted it all so? "Where did my dreams go? Where did life go?" they ponder. How many men and women every year take their wedding vows, thinking that in short order they will be before a court seeking a divorce—unable to look in the eye the one to whom they made all those promises after the affair?

None of us plans to fail. None of us intends to make small mistakes that turn into huge issues that ruin our lives, but those small mistakes happen. No sane person would want to put themselves in the unenviable position of Judas, and reap the rewards of eternal damnation. It nonetheless happens. The Bible tells us the reason Judas did his evil deed was due to the fact that *Satan entered into him*. Yet, as Paul lamented over engaging in the very practices he hated *(Rom. 7:15-22)*, he said, "I find then the principle that *evil is present in me*, the one who wishes to do good." Can any of us therefore honestly say we are immune to the deceptions of the flesh that brought about Judas' downfall?

While I do acknowledge that Judas was a very unique case, I also know that many who believe in Jesus share in his self-delusion. Otherwise, what would have led Paul to so firmly and clearly warn the Corinthians of the grave consequences for improperly partaking of the Elements? Jesus warned of the traps of self-deception, when he said not everyone who mouthed the words, "Lord, Lord," would enter the kingdom of heaven, but only those who did the will of His Father *(Matt 7)*. Sounds a bit like His message to the Laodiceans, doesn't it? Big words accompanied by little deeds? Judas no doubt said, "Lord, Lord" many times, but did deeds of selfishness and treachery anyway. How many who call themselves Christians fall squarely into that camp today? Everyone who is a sinner, and that is *everyone*.

Do We Betray the Son of Man With a Kiss?

I wonder, as I look upon the state of organized religion in America, if Jesus does not look down from heaven and pose the question to many who call Him Lord that He asked of Judas: "Do you betray the Son of Man with a kiss?" Would He ask, as Julius Caesar did of his good friend Marcus Brutus when he was stabbed to death by he and others who feigned allegiance, "Et tu [you too], My child?"

Sadly, modern day Communion services have become places where untold numbers come forth unworthily, if indeed a true self-exam is required. This is because most people lack a proper understanding of its glorious purpose, rather than being deceptive or rebellious as Judas was. It's because the truth isn't being taught. Our modern shepherds have made Communion a place to "kiss" the grace of Christ, but ignore the warnings of Christ.

He is not mocked. He sees into our hearts. His Table is the place where such betrayals and self-deceptions must stop. This is the place where those betraying the Son of Man in their lives, must be warned to use the occasion to repent, make amends, and come forward to find healing. As Jesus said to Judas that night that sealed both their fates, "Go and do what you do quickly."

I find it fascinating that our instruction in Matthew 5, and Christ's command to Judas, revealed the same urgency to *go with haste…quickly*, to act upon the revelation of God. We can either go with *urgency* in obedience to the Spirit and return ready to partake in victory, or like Judas we can go in obedience to the flesh and Satan, perhaps never to return with clean hands. We can either go and make amends for our sin, or go on in continued betrayal. Whatever our choice is to be, we are not to procrastinate.

> **Proceed to obedience or continue in betrayal, but no longer deceive yourself for even a moment.**

At the altar of Communion, Jesus calls for a quick and decisive end to our hypocrisy. The message? "No more denial, rationalization, or procrastination. Face the truth, and face it quickly. Proceed to obedience or continue in betrayal, but no longer deceive yourself for even a moment."

Communion is the place God has given us, that we might stop betraying Him with superficial kisses. It is the place where we can break the chain of poor choices that lead to a betrayal of Christ in our lives. It would be the Judas-killer, if our shepherds would but teach it properly and participants would but take it seriously, and employ it for its intended use.

Judas thought he could force Jesus to be what he thought Jesus should be. He thought he could mold Jesus into his own image of what he thought the Messiah should look like, and it cost him his eternal soul. How many today continue on in practiced, unrepentant sin, thinking God somehow overlooks it, or actually participates in it? How many today think they can mold Jesus into a god who blesses their habitual sin addictions? How many think that there will be no price to pay as they betray the Son of Man to their families, friends, and co-workers who are ultimately affected by the collateral damage that always accompanies such practices?

How many modern Judases will get to the end, and find out they have sold their souls for a few coins? How many will desire, when it's too late, to go back and change it? How many will be left with the terrifying and inescapable conclusion that they have spent a lifetime talking a good game, but mocking Christ's innocent blood shed for them? How many will have spent a lifetime saying, "Lord, Lord," even as they betrayed Him with their Sunday kisses—only to hear Him respond, "Depart from Me?"

How many modern Laodiceans are there, who think they are doing fine because they attend church regularly, enjoy good health, and prosper in the eyes of the world, when in fact their contribution to the body of Christ could be called *lukewarm* at best? Can we really examine poll after poll citing the lukewarmth of the vast majority of those who call themselves Christian, and not believe many follow closely the pattern set by Judas Iscariot? Too many keep up the appearance of following Jesus, when according to the polls their hearts are far from Him.

Don't get left standing outside the doorposts that are sprinkled with the Lamb's blood when the angel of weakness, sickness, and sleep passes by. Don't be dismissed from the Table for eternity because of continued betrayal of the Son of Man with meaningless kisses. Don't betray Jesus through a life of superficiality and lawlessness, all the while saying, "Lord, Lord" on Sundays.

And please don't fail to take this opportunity to examine yourself before you eat and drink…and this with the goal of a clear conscience both before God and man. Consider well weather you contribute to the body or hold it back, and allow yourself this marvelous opportunity to be judged righteously [by the fellowship] so that you won't be judged [by God]. Offer yourself to be disciplined by the Lord, in order that you may not be condemned along with the world *(1 Cor. 11:32)*.

Confess your sin to both God and man, and come humbly before the scrutiny of your heavenly Judge, and the human counselors He has put squarely in your path. Take action! Go with *urgency* to be reconciled with those you have harmed, *then* come back and present your offering. If God's people will just take advantage of this anointed tool for the maintenance of their faith, there will be a lot fewer Judases left hanging at the end of nooses of self-deception in that final day.

"Et tu, Judas?" This is a question none of us wants to hear at the judgment seat of Christ. Learn from the example of Judas, and don't let small, poor choices mature and grow into a practiced lifestyle of lawlessness. Join in both the joys *and* the responsibilities of the celebration of the Lamb of sacrifice regularly, and let Judas remain a singular pitiful legacy.

XIII. WALKING THROUGH A POWERFUL CEREMONY

If we're ever going to change the way Communion is done today, we simply must change the setting. Members of the Church in Acts 2 gathered day by day in the *temple*, but partook of Communion *house to house*. This method corresponds perfectly with Jesus' Passover, as at the time, He was *teaching daily in the Temple* in Jerusalem, but specifically selected the more intimate and private setting of the upper room for His Passover. Jesus still today has supremely important messages to convey to each and every one who participates, and that's impossible to do in 15 minutes shoehorned into the end of a Sunday service, with little or no time given to instruction, and none at all to interactive confession.

I believe Jesus knew that within the confines of a large group setting, where both believers and unbelievers would be in attendance, it would be impossible for future overseers to facilitate thorough self-exams, or help participants through their struggles. He also knew that people trapped in self-deceptive webs of sin would incur judgment upon themselves from a God they couldn't see, rather than embarrass themselves in the eyes of the people they could see. Brian Hathaway discusses what his church discovered concerning the proper environment for Communion in his insightful model for building a Christ-centered fellowship:

> One of the stumbling blocks for us in the breaking of bread service had been the linking of worship and Communion in the same service. *There is no Biblical precedent for this.* By separating these two activities it is possible to be much more flexible. We encourage people nowadays to take Communion together in home groups…In fact, it can be taken whenever Christians gather together. *It was birthed in relationships, and*

should be practiced in relationships. What was initially a simple act between the Lord and His disciples has, in many churches, become a ceremonial event...We moved to one all-in service on Sunday morning and put Communion into small groups, *which incidentally is where Jesus instituted it in the first place.*[emphasis mine] 46

Brian doesn't mention the original Passover of the Exodus, which also agrees with the home group model. It is interesting to note that the Old Testament model closely mirrors the new when it comes to the contrast between large and small group venues. According to historic accounts, certain notes called "work sheets" were carved into clay pots that have been unearthed. These notes were kept by the Egyptian slave-masters, to keep track of their Israelite workers. Some of these sheets were found to say:

> Most interesting are the entries for a man "offering to his god," or for the whole gang having several days off for a local religious festival. 47

Rameses II evidently sought to pacify his Jewish slave labor force by allowing limited larger group gatherings from time to time. When it came to Passover, however, God's people were specifically commanded to observe it with their families. This closely mirrors Jesus' treatment of His Passover. While the Jews eventually made it into a large group affair [as we have done again today] the small-group, house-to-house setting was the commanded model at the time it was instituted. As with all other things He made new, Jesus then restored Communion to its proper setting.

This begs the question why don't we follow more exactly the biblical model, and observe Communion house-to-house with our flesh and blood relatives? If Jesus wanted to follow the true Passover model, why not partake with His many relatives? He did, but in the Spirit the definition of the nuclear family as we would understand it changes. One of the many things Jesus came to give us was a new definition of the word *family*. In Matthew 12, He was speaking to a large crowd as

His mother and brothers stood outside seeking to speak to Him. When Jesus heard about this, He said, "Who is My mother, and who are My brothers?" He then stretched out His hand toward His disciples, and said, "Behold, My mother and My brothers! For whoever does the will of My Father who is in heaven, he is My brother and sister and mother."

Combine this with what Jesus said in Matthew 10, concerning turning a man against his father, and a man's enemies coming from the members of his blood relatives, and we find the bond of the Spirit is thicker than blood. A new *family* emerges—a family made up of spiritual brothers and sisters who belong through knowing Jesus, and doing His will. When Jesus chose those to share this most intimate of ceremonies with, He selected those who had left everything to follow Him. They were His new family, and their kinship in the Spirit was thicker than blood, as it is to this day.

> **Under the New Covenant, we can consider anyone who is joined with us in intimate fellowship our family.**

We can therefore consider anyone who is joined with us in intimate fellowship our family, even more so than our own flesh and blood. Therefore, in the Passover of the Exodus, the church of Acts, and Christ's Passover, we see a completely consistent biblical model of intimate small groups, coming together in the fellowship of the Holy Spirit, and gathering house-to-house.

Establishing an Environment

Considering the typical spontaneity of Jesus during His ministry, the meticulous preparations made at His behest for the Passover seem rather odd. Nowhere but here do we ever find Jesus sending the disciples before Him to prepare any venue of any kind. He typically preached from boats, in fields, and on mountaintops—inviting Himself to eat with anyone and everyone at a moment's notice. He was a self-proclaimed prophet who had nowhere to lay His head. Why then such elaborate preparation made here? Jesus desired just the right place and the proper setting for Him and His family on this, His last night of freedom. The message was far too important to share with those who heard only in parables. It was meant specifically, as it is today, for those He called *friend*.

Conversely, churches across America prepare meticulously for services every Sunday. Great pains are taken, and copious amounts of money spent, to make sure the worship music, lighting, sound, audio-visual presentations, the message, and all the various trappings of the sanctuary are spot-on. While I agree that believers ought always to seek for excellence in everything they do, when we examine the way Jesus and His staff of disciples typically held a church service, we find anything *but* careful planning.

His most famous sermon of all was *on the mount*, and who exactly was that usher who allowed a bunch of friends of a sick guy to climb up on a rooftop, remodel the church ceiling into a skylight, and lower down their friend on a pallet? Jesus' entire ministry was one of spontaneity and unpredictability. In fact, the only staff meeting to be found for any of Christ's church services was one hurriedly assembled to figure out how to feed over 5,000 people at a potluck, where the only one who must have read the invitation brought a lunch-pail with some bread and a few fish!

The question then arises: if we so meticulously prepare for services that Jesus was totally spontaneous about, what kind of effort should we expend to prepare for a ceremony He was so meticulous about? Forgive me if this sounds too much like a rigid list of do's and don'ts, but if Jesus was so particular about establishing a proper Communion setting at His Passover, perhaps we should be a little more careful to prepare ours.

> **If we so meticulously prepare for services that Jesus was fairly spontaneous about, what kind of effort should we expend to prepare for a service He was so meticulous about?**

In Preparation for the Ceremony

Here are a few suggestions to help facilitate an effective ceremony:

- ✦ Location: Gather at a neutral place—somewhere other than any of the participants' homes. This was Jesus' model for His

Passover. If one of the participants is also the host, they will be more likely focusing on hosting than in participating. It is best to gather in a getaway kind of place, where people unburdened with other responsibilities, and distanced from the rat race. A place that has numerous small areas of privacy, where two or three can gather together in confession and prayer, is ideal. This can be a borrowed cabin, a home, or—weather permitting—a campsite or other outdoor location where you can have a warm fire burning. If your "upper room" needs some cleaning or work to get it ready, do as Jesus did and have a couple of people go ahead to prepare it. You may want to spend the night, and if so bring the proper supplies for this.

Furthermore computers, cell phones, and pagers should be left at home, save possibly one brought along for emergencies. Get rid of any and all possible distractions, as Jesus did the night of His Passover. Many distractions are there as a part of the support system for those who want to avoid getting to the heart of their problems anyway.

+ Drive-time fellowship: Many times a drive of an hour or so to the location is a great way to spur conversation, and establish a natural state of fellowship. Carpool, so people are together, where they can interact within a critical social mass.

+ What to bring: Aside from those necessities involved in an overnight trip [if that's what you decide], only Bibles, a guitar [hopefully someone will be available to lead worship], and the Communion Elements should be included. This isn't a social event. Everyone should be well-fed beforehand, so perhaps you can stop and dine on the way to your destination. Paul addressed this specifically in his instructions to the Corinthians by telling anyone who was hungry to eat before they showed up.

+ Child care: Children and babies should be left with friends. If you have other small groups in your church, try to form teams that help each other with child care. Even if younger family members are old enough, and wish to participate, they

The Lost Supper

will inhibit the parents from fully engaging. Perhaps they could join with others of their peers in their youth group, also participating in Communion. My formative experiences with *The Lost Supper* were in a youth group setting. You will find that teenagers always adapt to changes that challenge traditional thinking far easier than adults do.

✦ Group size and make-up: I have found a group of eight to twelve to be ideal for this. If you have too few, some may feel you have failed to reach a critical mass, and to them this is important. Too many, on the other hand, will be difficult to shepherd, allowing those in denial the ability to do what they have been able to do so well in modern church observances: hide in crowds. Don't let this happen. These are the very ones that we must help to break the cycle of deceit and superficiality, and a small-group setting is where they can be challenged to stop the cover-up and participate.

I have also found the Lord's Table to be best split among the genders. What with the family dysfunction in the church today, the different issues men and women face, and how they approach them, confession comes far more easily with the sexes segregated. To this end, men's or women's retreats prove an excellent setting for a ceremony of this type. While there may be considerably larger numbers involved, an entire weekend setting in a getaway location is ideal. In such a venue there is plenty of time to break the teaching into

> **Give plenty of time. Do not attempt to muzzle this ox when he's on the threshing floor!**

segments, and the church small group leaders will probably be on hand when it's time to break up for discussion and the confessional.

✦ Time: Give plenty of time. When the Spirit moves as He will here, time must be granted, and control released to Him. Hurting and superficial people need to be given time to deal with sin, both before their brethren and God. Within reason, ample time needs to be allowed for the kind of individual prayer, confession, and fellowship that is critical to an effective self-examination process. Rob Bell says:

> What was the ritual the first Christians observed with the most frequency? Exactly. The common meal, also called the...Lord's Supper. And what did this meal consist of? Hours of talking and sharing and enjoying each other's presence...Time spent around the table with each other is time spent with God. 48

This is a time when the Holy Spirit moves powerfully in the lives of those who will invite it. Do not attempt to muzzle this ox when He's on His threshing floor! Just sit back and marvel at the work He does through this, that glorifies Him so!

✦ Frequency: You should only employ this in-depth ceremony three to four times per year. It should be special, and looked forward to with anticipation by the participants. Even though done infrequently, you will find an amazing thing will happen when *The Lost Supper* is fully experienced and understood within the small-group setting. Once people have witnessed the power of it, regular Communion services at church will take on new meaning and significance [see more on this in chapter XV]. The power of abstinence will be understood, and those who need will feel more naturally drawn to seek out others to confess to.

The Ceremony

Once the ceremony has begun, here are some suggestions for enhancing its effectiveness:

✦ Opening Worship: It is usually good to begin your time with an initial prayer from the small-group leader that begins challenging the group from the outset. While prayers should never be canned, the themes we've discussed to this point need to be maintained throughout by leaders on a mission to unleash Communion's power, and see results [consider praying an appropriate Psalm]. After this, it is most helpful to have someone in your group who can facilitate worship. Many people feel inhibited to sing a cappella, so a guitar would be helpful.

Worship has always been critical to entering into God's presence, because it facilitates so well the softening of hearts, and the opening of minds to the Holy Spirit's leading. Songs or Hymns should be focused on God, reverent, and simple—no complicated melody lines or lyrics that are hard to follow. Word sheets should be easily readable, with large type. No one should be confused by complicated hymns, or new songs they have never heard before. The ideal environment for worship facilitates a total focus upon God, with nothing else to distract.

Establishing fellowship is always made easier through an initial time of musical worship. There is a reason virtually all Sunday services since time began have started with singing of hymns or worship songs, and why there is so much evidence that God takes pleasure in worship throughout the Scriptures. Music soothes us, calms and focuses our hearts, and prepares our souls to accept the spoken word that is to follow. In the Passover accounts in Matthew, Mark, and Luke, Jesus set the tone by singing a hymn with His disciples.

✦ Washing feet: In the Gospel account of John, one of the first things Jesus did was to wash the feet of the disciples to show them that they were not to be masters, but servants of one another. This can be a wonderful way to relieve tensions new and different ideas always cause, and begin opening hearts to a radically different ceremony. May I suggest that the group's leader start this out, as did Jesus that fateful night? Ask one person to come forward, wash that person's feet, and say something edifying about or to them. Then invite someone else to take a shot at it with another they wish to edify.

Hopefully, this will become contagious to the rest of the group. If nothing else, it will establish the leadership as those unafraid to follow in the footsteps of Jesus, as they strive to make the Passover all it can be. Those observing will quickly see this will be a radically different affair than they have ever before experienced.

✦ Teaching: If Jesus found it so important to be teaching at the Passover [John 13-16], and Paul found it so important to teach specifics to the Corinthians, shouldn't we give thought to exact teaching during Communion services as well? The proper setting of the small group, outside of the restricting confines of church services, affords the time necessary to teach specifically about both the grace and the admonishments critical to fulfilling participation. God's word never returns to Him void. It does accomplish His purposes *(Isa. 55:11)*. This is one of the reasons I prefer "retreats" for Communion. It presents the opportunity to spend the evening teaching, and fully experiencing prayer and confession, with the opportunity to take the Elements the following morning. It gives people a chance to chew on what the Spirit is trying to accomplish in them while the lay down to sleep, and to consider well what to do with Matthew 5.

Teaching the truth with passion and conviction will give everyone gathered a thorough understanding of both the purpose and solemnity of the meal. As already discussed, Peter forewarned that people forget. The master deceiver is relentless in his attemps to put us to sleep to our sin.

> **Teaching needs to be done *every* time the Table is set, even for those who have heard it before.**

Therefore, the teaching needs to be done *every time*, even if abbreviated because everyone in the group has heard it before, to stir up their spirits and prepare them for what God would have them *there remember*. The truths of God's Word need to be spoken without fail every time the Table is set.

You will find an outline at the end of this chapter you can copy and use. Teach, of course, as the Spirit leads, but try to include most of the subjects on the outline. Of utmost importance is that everyone understands the concept of proactive seeking of God's conviction in prayer, the interactive healing confession of the saints, repentance through both words *and* deeds, and The Matthew 5 Alternative.

If you have read this material, believe it to be true, and God is nudging you toward a desire to share it with your group, then pay close attention to your homework, love your brothers and sisters, and trust in God to empower you to teach with conviction and passion. If you do, I guarantee you will see amazing results. I have never administrated over one of these ceremonies without marveling at what the Holy Spirit accomplishes in the lives of participants.

Prepare by reading John 13 through 17, and 1st Corinthians 11. Witness the passion Christ showed for this, His most holy moment with the disciples—His final briefing to his soldiers prior embarking upon their ultimate mission in life. Then seek Him in prayer for the wisdom, boldness, passion, and compassion you will need to facilitate His Spirit moving in your small group.

+ Prayer [vertical examination]: After the teaching, hand out the Prayer Recorders [or at the least paper and pens] and split the group up for about thirty minutes to let God examine them. Again, remind them this is a time to earnestly seek from the Spirit what David sought in Psalm 51: "Lord, examine my heart and see if there be any wicked ways in me." This is the time to open the door to the self-examination process through God's convictions. Suggest participants read the verses on the Recorder, and write down all that comes to their minds—no matter how trivial, irrelevant, or strange it may seem. Remind them also of Matthew 5, and that *here* is the place He will bring them to *remember* all the kingdom business that He wants them to attend to, as a part of worthy and transforming participation.

+ Small-group confession [horizontal examination]: After calling participants back from prayer, review the power of James 5.

Then split everyone into smaller groups and grant plenty of time to allow participants to confess the items they've written down to others, and to receive intercessory prayer on the spot. Everyone should feel free to move around from group to group as the Spirit leads, as long as they are not doing it to avoid confronting their sin. Instruct them that the confessional needs to be done in a spirit of both love and reverence, to keep focused on what they have just heard from God, and the power to carry out any tasks He has placed before them.

This is the place, and now is the time. This is the single most fruitful segment of the Communion ceremony, and will be the hardest to engage in for those who have been living lies and engaging in cover-ups. What happens during this phase will amaze you if the teaching is bold, the prayers fervent, and the leadership dedicated to reeling in the self-deceived.

✣ The end gathering: After sufficient time has been given to the confessional process, call the group back together to partake of the Elements [unless it is an overnight stay, in which case I would suggest waiting until morning]. Some groups may have to be cut short, but encouragement can be given to them to continue at a later time. Once gathered, again stress there are dire consequences for partaking unworthily, and that you, as their shepherd who loves them, would hate to see any in your care go on suffering needlessly. Remind them also that The Matthew 5 Alternative is the way to safely proceed, if they have any questions at all concerning their thoughts and conduct. Here, like nowhere else, it is better to be safe than sorry. We will *never* be condemned for abstaining, even if our reasons for doing so may, in retrospect, have been found to be wrong. Discretion here is certainly the better part of valor.

Finally, admonish all that every participant's decision made in honesty and humility should be a cause for rejoicing—whether it be to partake or abstain. Paul said that whether we *eat or drink*, or in whatever else we do, to do all of it to God's glory *(1 Cor. 10:31)*. Reiterate that the goal is being real with Jesus and oneself. For those who feel the Spirit is prompting them to abstain at this time, the goal is to share the victory of Matthew 5 the next time you gather. Remind everyone of their Great Commandment obligation to follow up where help is needed, give those abstaining encouragement that they will be supported throughout the process, and that the group will be living for the day that they gain victory over their roadblocks. After this lead the group in a prayer of thanksgiving, bless the Elements, and pass them out. This will complete the celebration.

Another of the twelve steps warrants repeating here concerning the repetitive nature of Communion that provides for the regular maintenance of our spiritual and emotional health:

> We continued to take personal inventory, and when we were wrong promptly admitted it. 49

Every time we approach the Lord's Table is a renewed opportunity to continue to take personal inventory, and when we are wrong promptly go back through the process of participatory confession and repentance. Once we understand the true nature of why God gave us this ceremony, we are constantly reminded of the need to pull a brother or sister aside, confess our sins, and begin the process anew. And we don't have to even wait for Communion to do that.

House-to-house, Communion provides an environment thoroughly conducive to intimacy, and to confronting sin and superficiality in the lives of all participants. If we fail to confront and deal with sin, and thus fail to derive from the process a *true* appreciation of grace, the Communion Table has failed to produce its most desired fruit. If people are allowed to flunk their self examination and

> **If we fail to confront and deal with sin, the Communion Table has failed to produce its most desired fruit.**

partake anyway, the reason for the ceremony turns from healing to self-destruction. God's judgment is incurred, and not His grace, if this most holy of moments is allowed to be used to cover up sin rather than expose and deal with it. Spiritual weakness, sickness, and sleep are *sure* to follow.

If an environment is established where self-examination is less intimidating, and the love necessary to clear the hurdles it presents more available, this is far less likely to occur. So prepare well and meticulously, as Jesus did that fateful night. Your group of disciples, like His, will go forth into the great adventure of the faith bright-eyed and bushy-tailed, healed, and ready to go forth on their mission in Christ.

XIV. A FEW FINAL CONSIDERATIONS

In addition to the worthiness of the individual's ability to participate in the Lord's Table, there are a few other issues to consider as, and after, you gather:

Gossip

Though we've gone beyond all reasonable constraints concerning confidentiality in the church, the damage gossiping can do—not only to the victims, but to those who spread it—can be immense. Discuss verses like Proverbs 13:3 and Romans 1:28-31, to help the group understand that those who hear confessions need to be mature, and careful about spreading what they have heard beyond reasonable boundaries. The Bible seems to indicate that two or more is a sufficient number in the arbitration and establishment of answers to most of our important issues.

On the evidence of two or more witnesses, people were convicted or exonerated *(Deut. 17:6)*, matters were confirmed or denied *(Deut. 19:15)*, facts were confirmed for the confrontation of the self-deceived *(Matt. 18, 2 Cor. 13)*, and accusations were accepted or rejected *(1 Tim. 5)*. Matthew 18 tells us that where two or more are gathered together, Jesus is present among them. It would seem a good number, then, that two or more would be a standard for most confessions. We must question, then, why anyone would refuse to confess to a small group of intimately acquainted spiritual family members that would be gathered before the Lord's Table.

I wish that we all enjoyed the freedom, and had the courage to openly confess our sins, but love demands those more mature must be mindful of the maturity of those less mature. We cannot force maturity by forcing all confessions into plains too broad for others to handle. If someone has heard a confession, and thereafter wishes to seek more help to deal with the confessor or the problem, he or she should first gain the confessor's permission before sharing the issue with someone outside the immediate group that was brought into confidence. Fellowship can easily be destroyed, and your small group can be made a place of strife and distrust, if the members betray confidences without permission.

Too many times confessions have been made only to be betrayed by loose lips, causing the church to turn to the professional-client model of Christian therapy that, while ensuring confidentiality, undermines fellowship. If gossip is a temptation for you, simply treat it as you would any other sin at the Table. Make it a confession of your own, and allow the group to pray for you, and hold you accountable to displaying reasonable discretion. Don't take private confessions beyond the reasonable boundaries that facilitate healing over issues revealed during Communion.

Making Promises

Making a Communion commitment is to make a realistic personal commitment to act or to change, rather than making vows to God or anyone else. Jesus warned that we were to make no oaths at all, but to let our statement be a simple "yes" or "no." Anything beyond this He said would be evil *(Matt. 5)*. James echoed this admonishment, and forewarned we would fall under God's just judgment if we did *(Jas. 5:37)*.

We are to be men and women of our word, and let our deeds speak louder than our lips if we want to display true integrity. It is to be about changing who we truly are, rather than speaking vainly about who we hope we can be. The message? It is better to make no

> **Commitments are to be about changing who we truly are, not speaking vainly about whom we hope we can be.**

promises at all, than to make and then break them, because our sinful nature predisposes us to do the latter.

Therefore, when it concerns Communion responsibilities, simply make the commitment to yourself, and verbalize it to God and the fellowship by saying something like, "by His power working in me,

I will do my best to..." and then let your yes be yes by acting on that commitment. Promises made, and then not kept, become lies. They then inevitably lead to self-delusion and superficiality, as the mind is forced to try to rationalize the disconnection between words and actions. Refuse to ask for, or give, any oaths concerning what you or anyone else will or will not do. If another participant is in to making promises, remind them of Jesus' words, and encourage them to just go do whatever it is they are promising to do.

Causing Stumbling

The vast majority of churches in America invite anyone to this ceremony openly, or by omission fail to warn the unbeliever [or the believer with a heart hardened to sin], to consider abstinence from the Elements. It is a sad fact that most administrators of the Table today end their Communion instruction with the first three verses in 1st Corinthians 11, and totally ignore the rest. In fact, the heresy has advanced to the point that many say nothing at all. They place the elements in the corners of the sanctuary, and invite both believer and unbeliever alike to go forth into judgment whenever they want, and under any conditions they desire. There is no warning at all, nor is there any discussion of the meaning of the most important and holy ceremony of the New Testament.

When those who are supposed to lead disallow the Holy Spirit His ability to work in the hearts of His children gathered around the Table [by refusing to at the very least read Paul's entire instruction in 1st Corinthians 11], they shirk their ultimate responsibility. They lead their flocks into the just judgment of God, rather than His grace as they suppose. How can they possibly do such a thing in the name of the very love the Table should be about?

Do those in your church who administer the Lord's Sacraments even read the total account in 1st Corinthians 11, much less teach it? How many of the saved do you see abstain because they realize there is urgent kingdom business Matthew 5 would tell them they need to *quickly* attend to? Likewise, how many whom you know to be unbelievers, or very unsure of where they stand with God, go forward blindly?

What is a person to do when the warnings are absent? Is he or she to partake, even if found to be personally worthy? While many may think me legalistic for this, I believe there to be an issue rather of love that would lead me to say that such a one, even if personally prepared, should abstain from any Communion where the warnings are ignored. It is for this reason I rarely partake in modern church ceremonies. Let me explain.

Paul's exhortations concerning each in Christ regarding others as more important than themselves *(Phil. 2:3)*, are taken seriously by those truly led by God's love. They understand Paul's heartfelt anxieties over the struggles of others, as he asks, "Who is led into sin without my intense concern" *(2nd Cor. 11)*? Likewise, we observe Paul's passionate joy in the maturing faith of his children, in 1st Thessalonians 2 and 3: "For you [our disciples] are our glory and joy... now we really live, if you stand firm in the Lord!" When one becomes a conduit of Christ's love, one loses all concern for oneself and grows beyond such selfish desires. By love's definition in 1st Corinthians 13, one becomes ultimately concerned for giving all, and keeping nothing.

> **When one becomes a conduit of Christ's love, one loses all concern for oneself, and has grown beyond selfishness.**

Out of this same love of Christ that directed his steps, Paul spoke of how *our* conduct was to be directed to an extent by concern over our weaker brothers *(1st Cor. 13:22-23)*. He said that we were to refuse to partake in something that caused the confused and less mature to stumble, even if it was acceptable behavior for us. Was Paul being *legalistic* here? In his own words: "May it never be!" This is love that transcends self—the love of Jesus—in action! Paul obviously took his own advice, and counted the needs of others as more important than his own.

Like Christ, he never wavered from his responsibility to place those put in his care before himself. He never stopped teaching, took every opportunity to model his own instructions, and was constantly concerned in every circumstance about the proper discipling of his flock. He came, like Jesus, to serve and not to be served. He loved those he led, and realized that different levels of maturity would always be an issue in the body. He didn't want the mature, who had reached a deeper understanding, doing anything through ignorance that would cause those less mature to stumble.

With a clear understanding of the solemn nature of the Altar, what do we think Paul would do concerning the personal participation of which we now speak? Would he take every opportunity to transform God's truths into daily opportunities for practical biblical obedience? Those more mature always have a responsibility to help lead less-mature brothers and sisters into the truth, and free them from stumbling. Enabling others to continue on in sinful patterns of self-deception is to do the opposite. It is to make them *stumble*.

If I find myself at a Communion service, where I can't possibly know the hearts of everyone in attendance, what am I doing by partaking when the Communion warnings are ignored? What if there be a man or woman next to me who is a believer, yet denying the Holy Spirit's convictions because of a heart hardened through perhaps years of rationalized disobedience? Will they not see me and everyone else partaking, and feel comfortable to join in regardless of their circumstances? Will they not feel the peer pressure to partake, when they know they shouldn't? Will they then go forward to incur judgment, ignorant of both the warnings and the consequences?

I've seen people time and time again who had to be dragged to church, and who admittedly didn't believe in God, partake in Communion without giving it a second thought. How can anyone who loves them, and truly cares for their soul, participate in this?

If Christ's love is abiding in me, and that makes *them* of far more value to me than I am to myself, don't I then partake selfishly by only thinking of my qualifications? Is this then love, as I perhaps cause this weaker one to stumble? It pains me to rarely be able to enter into Holy Communion in the church today, but I'd rather die than lead so many to stumble into the weakness, sickness, and spiritual sleep they now abide in.

> **This is not an issue of legalism, but of love! Are we concerned first for ourselves, or for our weaker members for whom Christ died?**

So I ask again, is this an issue of legalism or love? Are we concerned first for ourselves, or for our weaker members for whom Christ died?

Do we see to our own comforts in the body and blood of the Lord, as His bride continues on mired in her malaise?

Sondra was a young lady who spent many years in our small group. She was the kind of mature believer everyone looked up to. After she attended several Communion ceremonies with us, she came to me one day concerned about her church, because her pastor never proclaimed any of Paul's warnings when administering the Table. I encouraged her to speak to him about it, and asked her to consider how her participation might impact others around her.

Being the dedicated child of God she was, she took this to heart. She was afraid to confront him, but she chose the next best thing, and just quietly abstained the next time Communion was administered. When the service was over, Sondra's pastor approached her to inquire as to why she had abstained. She humbly explained to him her concerns for making her weaker brothers and sisters stumble. At first he was offended, and began defending his position. She came back to me with his arguments, we discussed them, looked at the scriptures, reinforced her resolve, and she stepped back into the fray.

Over time he came to acknowledge, albeit lukewarmly, her point. He grudgingly began to read the entire account in 1st Corinthians when administering Communion. She rejoiced in the fact that her resolve to fight for what she considered to be right would now result in her congregation at least being given an opportunity to hear the whole word of God.

An Opportunity to Witness

When we choose to abstain from the Table because the admonishments are passed over, we can effect positive change in the way it is done. We can also be led into opportunities to evangelize or disciple those in the congregation who would ask us why—and they do ask why. I have seen the unsaved witnessed to when their believing friends abstained, and asked why. I have many times seen believers living in superficiality challenged when they asked why.

It is a truly odd occurrence in our day and age, to see one who is an acknowledged disciple abstain from the Elements. When was the last time you observed this in any church? When was the last time you were the courageous one who counted your relationship with

God, and your love for your spiritual family, more important than your own participation? Yet, I would submit that if more believers understood the power, consequences, and promises involved in the Communion experience, things would change. When disciples abstain people occasionally ask why, and that is a question that always opens up the door to evangelism or discipleship.

Consider your ultimate mandate—the Great Commandment—to love, and always put others before self in all of these issues, and you will do well. Confront one another always in humility and love, as one sinner to another, be diligent to follow up on your responsibilities as you bear another's burdens, and the results will amaze you. Communion was intended for our healing, but if we don't pay close attention to ourselves and to our teaching in the interest of insuring both our own, and our brother's, salvation *(1 Tim. 4:16)* the power of it will be compromised. Remember that, with Jesus, it's never about us. It's always and forever about sacrificing our own desires to see to the benefit of those He has given us to love.

XV. BRINGING IT BACK TO THE CHURCH

Communion can be experienced to an extent in a large group, after a proper understanding and reverence for it is developed in the small group. In the Passover of the Exodus, families were allowed to join together if neither one was large enough to fully consume their sacrificial lamb. There would also need to be room within the larger families for those individuals without families, and we do find in later accounts many instances of the Jews celebrating larger-scale Passovers. This leads me to wonder: was it because they wandered from the original model then, as we have wandered from Christ's original model today?

Inasmuch as small group Communion services should not be overdone, mixing them with larger group ceremonies is necessary to keep recognizing and dealing with destructive sin patterns on the front burner, as we seek to follow Jesus. Note as we walk through a truly blessed one found in 2nd Chronicles 30, that regardless of the size of the gathering, God's message for us in both Passover and Communion accounts has remained the same from the beginning.

To set the stage, Hezekiah had assumed the reins of power in Israel. Among the many godly reforms he institutes is a reinstatement of the Passover. Hezekiah sends out couriers with a decree that all the people of the land should come to Jerusalem and partake of the celebration, with the following invitation:

> Now do not stiffen your neck like your fathers, but yield to the Lord, and enter His sanctuary which He has consecrated forever. Serve the Lord your God that His burning anger may turn away from you *(vs. 8)*.

I have discussed at length, the dangers of coming to the Lord's Table with a hard heart. There is no place for those who refuse to yield to the

Spirit's convictions, humble themselves, and partake of the Elements as utterly repentant sinners. Our leaders today encourage us to come in any way we see fit, with little or no information given as to what coming with "stiff necks" means. Therefore, many come forward ignorantly and unworthily.

> For if you return to the Lord, your brothers and your sons will find compassion before those who led them captive, and will return to this land. For the Lord your God is gracious and compassionate, and will not turn His face away from you if you return to Him *(vs. 9)*.

Like the Prodigal Son discussed earlier, the purpose of Communion is to allow the prodigals that we all become at times to return to the Lord. If we will but consider our ways, and change our minds, He will always be gracious and compassionate. Jesus Christ is ever the merciful, forgiving Lord of all prodigals. There is no sin He will refuse to extend His loving kindness to cover, save blasphemy of the Spirit. If we say it is the hard heart of the unsaved that is blasphemous to the Spirit that convicts us of sin, could we also say that it would be the hard heart of the saved that would blaspheme by refusing the correction and training of that same Spirit: the One called *Teacher*?

What is blasphemy of the Holy Spirit, other than a heart hardened toward His correction and teaching at any time during our pilgrimage on earth? It is no coincidence then, that a hard heart is the very thing that *does* preclude us from the Table. However, when we return in true repentance by exposing our sin to God and man, the body broken for us and the blood poured out for us become more real and gracious than we can ever know.

> So the couriers passed from city to city through the country…but [some] laughed them to scorn, and

mocked them. Nevertheless, some men ... humbled themselves and came to Jerusalem *(vs. 10-11)*.

As has always been the case, there are those that will come to the Table mocking the Lord's convictions, with their indifference and willful unworthiness. There are also those who will come humbled and contrite in spirit. It is up to courageous leaders who take their calling seriously to admonish the hypocrites to repent or abstain, and encourage the humble to joyfully partake. The rest must be left in the hands of the Judge of men's souls. Our story continues:

> The hand of God was also on Judah, to give them one heart to do what the king and the princes commanded by the Word of the Lord *(vs. 12)*.

When we properly teach, properly observe, and give God the fear due Him at Communion, His hand will be with us. We will come together with one heart and one mind, like the Church of Acts as they broke bread. What could more surely accomplish one heart among the fellowship than the confession of all known sin, intercession, and action on the part of the individual and the fellowship? Communion can reunite hearts among any body of believers.

> And [the people] arose and removed the altars which were in Jerusalem. They also removed all the incense altars and cast them into the brook Kidron *(vs. 14)*.

This is proactive repentance! This is putting feet on a verbal commitment, which transforms mere words of sorrow into deeds that testify to true repentance. The people had kingdom business to attend to, *before* they came and presented their offering upon the altar. They *there remembered* that God had something against them. They did their business with haste, and; then presented their offering in true victory. The Matthew 5 Alternative! Oh, don't miss how this marvelous tool works to honor God, and cleanse the fellowship from sin and superficiality!

> Then they slaughtered the Passover Lambs *(vs.15)*.

Then, and only *then*, did they slaughter the Lamb! It is only after we partake of participatory repentance that we may come and partake of the slaughtered Lamb of God: the body broken and the blood poured out. It is only prodigals that return to their senses, repent, and confess their sin to their heavenly Father who will find Him waiting with rings for their fingers, sandals for their feet, and the slaughtered calf for their renewal! Hezekiah's people knew that until they had torn down the strongholds of sin in their kingdom, they couldn't enter into the Passover celebration. Until we likewise tear down, confront, confess, and act upon the strongholds of sin in our own lives, our worthiness to partake of the slaughtered Lamb of God at the Table of self-examination will be judged harshly by the God jealous for its purity. We will continue to be as far too many are today: thieves of grace.

> And the priests and Levites were ashamed of themselves, and consecrated Themselves…And they stood at their stations after their custom…The priests sprinkled the blood which they received from the hand of the Levites, for there were many in the assembly who had not consecrated themselves. Therefore, the Levites were over the slaughter of the Passover Lambs for everyone who was unclean, in order to consecrate them to the Lord. For a multitude of the people…had not purified themselves, yet they ate the Passover otherwise than prescribed *(vs. 16-18)*.

Shepherds of Christ's flock, do you hear it? Stand at your stations according to the 1st Corinthians instruction, and watch over those who have failed to consecrate themselves via a thorough self-exam. There is such a dire need today for leaders fully aware of their own sin, yet able to see the call of God clearly, to stand firm at their stations of responsibility in order to insure their flocks come worthily before the Altar.

There will always be people, at many stages of maturity, who won't understand the power of Communion to either heal or cause sickness—to bring God's blessing or His judgment. If courageous teachers would bear witness to the whole truth, in an effort to see their flocks cleansed and healed—if they would take seriously the power for good or destruction this single opportunity presents, I am wholly convinced that we would begin to turn the tide on this accursed sleep that has overcome the church in America. If godly administrators are disobedient to their command to stand boldly at their stations, confused people will continue to eat the Passover in ways *other than prescribed*. Hezekiah's story concludes:

> But Hezekiah prayed for them, saying, "May the good Lord pardon everyone who prepares his heart to seek God, the Lord God of his fathers, though not according to the purification rules of the sanctuary." So the Lord heard Hezekiah and healed the people *(vs. 18-20)*.

It is the duty of every facilitator of God's Holy Communion to be wary at all times of the stragglers: of those who cannot wean themselves from the milk of Christianity's teachings. Though they may have converted, they still hear God speak in parables. These need our special attention and our prayers, as they skate around the Table on very thin ice. It is all we can do to teach faithfully, love fully, and pray earnestly. Beyond that it is God's to convict and to judge, and each participant's choice to repent and partake, or abstain. We can only teach, love, and exhort with great patience and instruction, and pray. If shepherds do their jobs faithfully, God will see to His end of the bargain. Remember what James said about the fervent prayers of a righteous man accomplishing great things.

Training Worthy Administrators

Once people understand the power of the Table, and what role they play, small group or large they will never again view Communion in the same way. The blending of the two can be accomplished, if the church trains worthy leaders, commits to small-group fellowships, and makes them the training grounds for the ceremony. Sheep will always follow their shepherds.

> **Once people understand the power or the Table, and what role they play, they will never again view Communion in the same way.**

Therefore, small group leaders need to walk the walk of transparency and integrity before their flocks on a regular basis, so that they can react to Communion's formidable challenges with wisdom, competence, grace, and integrity. They need to be able to say before their groups at the Lord's Table what Paul said to his, "Be imitators of me, just as I am also of Christ" *(1 Cor. 11:1).* They must stop looking at themselves as mere teachers, and start seeing themselves as shepherds who lead not only with their words, but with their lives as well.

As a part of their training, pastors should celebrate *The Lost Supper* with them before they go forward to lead their groups through it. This will provide an ideal boot camp, as they will get to experience firsthand the fears and the joys of Communion, raise the questions they themselves will be confronted with, see the community fostered there for their encouragement, and understand fully what they will be asking of their fellowships. Then they will be able to understand and teach the warnings and encouragements necessary to unleash the power of Communion.

Bringing the various small groups together for unified church Communion could be a marvelous venue for testimonies to the power of the Lord and His most holy Table, but it must first be understood in the small group setting through the righteous teaching and example of dedicated small group shepherds.

Slaughtering Some Sacred Cows

One Sunday prior to Communion, the pastor gave a very convicting, on-target sermon on busyness. He hit all the bases: work, kids' sports, personal pleasure, and hobbies. He then gave us some time to quietly reflect on areas of our lives where busyness might be getting in the way of our relationship with God, and asked us to write them down. He said he was doing this because Communion was to be observed that following week, asked us to bring our notes then and he would tie it all together. I thought, "Wow, this is going to be great!" It seemed someone was finally going to use the Table of the Lord as intended. Hopefully, he was going to bring up his convicting message about busyness, and use the Table to challenge us to act upon our convictions. Someone was actually going to have the guts to require that we examine ourselves before partaking of the Elements. What a concept!

I eagerly anticipated that next week, because this was not a church given to convicting Communion ceremonies. I came expecting a breakthrough service, but it was not to be. He barely mentioned his challenge of the prior Sunday, his Communion teaching ended without mention of any warnings, and he waxed poetic about the Table being all about grace and forgiveness—as usual.

It will do no good to attempt to institute Communion effectively, if we don't change some popular theologies and denominational rules that now stifle it. The first is the ideal of costless grace [see my book: *Running the Race Already Won* for a more complete discussion of this subject]. In the first chapter of his book *The Cost of Discipleship*, Dietrich Bonhoeffer says:

> Cheap grace is grace we bestow on ourselves. Cheap grace is the preaching of forgiveness without requiring repentance, baptism without church discipline, Communion without confession, and absolution without personal confession. Cheap grace is grace without discipleship, grace with without the Cross, and grace without Jesus Christ living and incarnate…***the word of cheap grace has been the ruin of more Christians than any commandment of works.*** [emphasis mine]50

Jesus referred to Himself as Judge, as well as Savior. He is *both* Lamb of God, and King of kings. He is described by John as the One who came full of grace *and* truth *(John 1)*. We have endangered the concept of costly grace by extracting grace from truth, and truth from Christ. We have removed one part from the whole character of God, fashioned it as an idol, and now bow to it. It has become, as Bonhoeffer forewarned, a grace that we bestow upon ourselves, and call upon whenever we need it to make us feel better apart from true repentance.

The teaching of costless grace, so endemic in the modern church, has reaped untold cases of weakness, sickness, and sleep through unworthy participation in the Lord's Table. It has truly become the ruin of more Christians over the past century than any command of works. Poll after poll over the past 50 years reveal the church's pitiful record concerning the "making of disciples who *observe all* Jesus commanded," which is the

The Lost Supper

Great Commission. How can we be happy with this record? We harvest generations of *babes* and spectators, largely due to the confusing message of costless grace we are preaching. It is at the root of our Laodicean existence in the church in America.

When we read from the Word of God, it reaches into our hearts and requires some response from us. It requires our Amen with more than mere words. It *requires* change in our lives. The Word of God: living, active, sharp—piercing to the very depths of our souls, and able to judge the thoughts and intentions of the heart *(Heb. 4:12)*—profoundly impacts us. It *demands* real and practical application from us. Therefore, when we preach and teach this Word, but then suggest that it's really unnecessary to follow with life-application because grace covers all, we preach a message that *asks for everything while demanding nothing*.

This is a complete contradiction to the life and message of the One who came as the Word in the flesh, and thus very confusing to our flocks. The very leaders who preach the Word full of grace and command are the very ones who then tell us the command doesn't matter. The message of that pastor, who presented the challenge concerning busyness? "You really need to stop being so busy with worldly pursuits, but if you want to remain disobedient and lukewarm in your relationship with God, because you have no time for Him as you chase all of your selfish desires, don't worry about it. Hallelujah, grace has you covered!"

In 1 Samuel 24, David is told by God to go to a place owned by a man named Araunah, to offer up a sacrifice in order that a prophesied plague might be averted. When David tells Araunah why he has come, the man tells David to take whatever he likes at no charge. It is then we see a *heart after God's own* revealed, as David replied, "No, but I will surely buy it from you for a price, for I will not offer burnt offerings to the Lord my God which cost me nothing." Oh, that we would have the same wisdom when it comes to the Lord's Holy Communion! Oh, that we would stop presenting offerings to the Lord our God that cost us nothing! Grace is free, but it is not costless! There's a difference between the two, and it is the difference between healing and sickness at the Lord's Table. Grace wasn't costless to Jesus, and it isn't to us.

> **More than any other Christian activity, Communion absolutely demands something of us.**

More than any other activity we partake in as believers, Communion absolutely demands something of us. It *demands* that we take a piercing, critical, and typically chaotic look at ourselves—and ask the Spirit to do likewise. Communion *demands* that we answer the question, "Do I forsake all else to follow Jesus?" It *demands* that we answer the question, "Do I sell all I have to buy that extraordinary Pearl of Great Price?" It *requires* that we answer the question, "Am I a disciple who observes all Jesus commands? or a babe who says, 'Lord, Lord,' and yet do not do what He says?"

When we read God's Communion instructions, and become convicted within our spirit that they demand something of us, but then do nothing because we've been led to believe grace is costless, superficiality and hypocrisy are the inevitable result. Our actions don't line up with our convictions, and spiritual weakness and sickness follow. Until we abandon this practice, and require in our preaching and teaching what God clearly demands with His Word, the true power of Communion will go on drowning in a tepid, lukewarm sea of command without requirement, and grace without truth. It will continue to be the toothless placebo it has become in the modern church.

Decrees and Degrees of Men

If the administration of Communion is to be returned to its rightful hands, we must begin challenging unbiblical denominational rules and regulations forbidding lay leaders to oversee it. If the small-group philosophy is embraced, then the small-group leaders are the natural choice to administer the Elements. They are the ones who should have earned the privilege to facilitate the ceremony. They are the ones who will be in charge of seeing that follow-up is performed, and they will be the ones ultimately responsible for the overall spiritual health of their *families*.

There simply is no biblical support for restricting the administration of the Elements to ordained ministers. God entrusted His church to twelve men, none of whom had seminary degrees or ordination. In fact, the only one of Christ's disciples or apostles who had a seminary degree was Paul, and isn't it interesting that he was the only one who had to be literally blinded before he could see the truth?

Replacing God's liberties with men's laws in this fashion was precisely what elicited Christ's ire towards the Pharisees. It is just this type of yoke of human ordination superseding God's anointing they burdened the people with. It kept the laity from enjoying the true participatory experience of faith God had for them. These, whom Jesus rightly called *hypocrites*, set up a ruling class in the synagogue. Their message? "You must come through us to approach God. We are the ones in the know because of our great learning in the classrooms of man. We are the only ones worthy because of our degrees. You can't possibly understand His truths without being trained and watched over by us."

The administration of the Elements, like all other gifts from God, is a matter of divine calling upon men's hearts. It is men who desire to only make it available through the decree or degree of religious institutions. If the small-group leader doesn't feel called to administer the Elements, let him choose another from the group who does and let him see to it. Even in this case, the first leader should handle the teaching and oversight, because they alone have earned the right through enduring and faithful ministry to those participating.

The Bible is filled with stories of God using ordinary men and women to accomplish extraordinary things, while He rejected those who thought they were worthy simply because they considered themselves decreed and degreed by men. I am not recommending the selection of those to lead Communion be done without thought to their qualifications whatsoever, but those credentials need to come in the form of spiritual credibility and divine appointment. Overseers and Deacons have clearly set forth guidelines of character and conduct in the New Testament, and nowhere within them is that a man be ordained by anyone save the Spirit. Jesus rejected the seminarian's degrees, while going to those whose hearts would be open to divine appointment.

James warned that we should be extremely careful about considering our calling to become teachers. Those who do, set themselves up for a *stricter judgment* from God *(Jas. 3:1)*. Paul told his disciple Timothy to commit the truths of God to *faithful men,* who would be able to teach others also *(2 Tim. 2:2)*. These biblical guidelines need to be the model for the selection of small-group leaders, and are fully sufficient to qualify administrators of the Table.

If people have shown themselves to be worthy small-group shepherds, and are properly trained, and feel called to administer the Table, it is good enough. A seminary degree or church ordination, without being called of God and having earned the right through faithful ministry, should never qualify anyone to engage in such critical activities. Leaving Communion's administration in the hands of evangelists ordained to preach and teach amongst large gatherings, rather than those ordained to nurture and disciple within small groups, is part of what has brought us to the impotent state of Communion ceremonies today.

> A seminary degree or church ordination, without a calling and earning of the right through faithful ministry, should never qualify anyone to administer the Lord's Table.

If denominational boundaries prohibit lay pastors from administering the Sacraments, may I suggest you have faithful men installed as elders and deacons, who are also your small-group leaders. If all else fails, you can have someone who is ordained come join you at the Table to administer the Elements. However, the small-group leader should still teach and oversee all activities. If even this is disallowed, perhaps a new denominational alliance is in order. Such Pharisaical, unbiblical, stifling policies must not be allowed to suffocate the clearly established house-to-house participation upon which God's church, and Christ's Passover, was founded.

If a true house-to-house philosophy is established as the foundation of church community, then this intimate model of Communion will be a natural fit. If unbiblical religious models prohibit it, then find a new church home. Observances of the Table aside, not much of any real growth medium will be there for people in a church that has a weak, or nonexistent small-group ministry. Small groups are where we engage in *practicing* what we learn. Small-group discipleship is the way Jesus trained up His followers from babes to meat-eaters, and it has been His model ever since. It was His small group He chose for the Passover, and we must return to that model if Communion is to be any different, or more effective, than the fifteen-minute powerless ceremonies we now vainly pursue.

Communion *can* be blended back into the large group setting. But it must be taught and experienced *first* within the discipleship setting. This can be done if we stop preaching costless grace, put Communion back into the environment it was born in, and challenge unbiblical philosophies and regulations that now stifle its power to heal.

XVI. IT'S UP TO YOU NOW

I am reminded of a speaker I used to hear at youth camps in Colorado. His trademark summation on the last night was to apologize to those who refused the extended hand of Jesus. He would tell the young people gathered that they would now have no excuse for rejecting God as they stood before Him on the final day of their life, because he had fully and clearly explained the Gospel to them.

I would now ask you, what would keep you from employing this marvelous gift of God to break the spell of the superficiality the polls tell us so clearly exists in the church? I have done my best to explain fully to you, the reader, both the dangers of continued wrongful participation, and the joys and benefits of experiencing the cleansing and healing that awaits all who will follow the biblical model. Will you be a part of renewal, or continue to submit to the status-quo?

Through His death, resurrection, and example set in His Passover, Jesus has placed a miraculous gift in our hands. The question becomes, will we unwrap it? It's up to you now. What will you do? If you've come this far, and still think 15 minute rituals packed into the end of Sunday services—with little time for teaching, and no time for self-examination or confession—is what God intended, then by all means don't employ *The Lost Supper*. But if you know in your spirit that this is right, then hear the words of James when he says it is sin for the one who knows the right thing to do, and fails to do it *(Jas. 4:17)*.

This ultimate ceremony of fellowship, full of the awesome power of the conviction of the Holy Spirit, and the grace of the crucified Christ, refuses to allow those who partake to sit on the fence of neutrality. They will either be *for Jesus,* and both allow and participate in a full self-exam, or they will be *against Him* as they perpetuate cover-ups, and succumb to the storms of life. Those who are *for* Jesus in this matter will help those in their care face a reality that few in Christianity now grasp. How can that be a bad thing? Simply ask yourself how your spirit reacts to the current way it is done. Do you feel the power of life and death in it, or not? Do you walk away from modern observances transformed, or feeling a temporary and fleeting well-being?

Communion provides an environment uniquely conducive to growing us into true disciples, or exposing us as posers if we continue to choose rationalization and denial. It is God's regular and gracious gift to get to the root of sin with the help of the body, and then deal with it. Or it is His tool of judgment. It can be the ultimate gift for the fellowship seeking sanctification, through the washing and renewal that the Spirit can so fully bring *(Tit. 3:15)*. It can also be the ultimate glue to bond our fellowships in Christian love, the power of confession, prayer, and accountability.

God's Holy Communion is an environment where men and women can regularly wrestle with sin, and by doing so can gain the *blameless conscience* before God and man Acts speaks of. It is an environment where believers can proactively attack Satan's deceptions that are controlling their lives. It is a place

> **This incredible, masterful, divine gift is the very culture God ordained to transform the difficult processes of sanctification into imminently doable reality.**

where divine plan, self-examination, prayer, and confession lead to a far deeper relationship between a believer and God than they knew before. It is where we are brought to *remember* real work is to be done, and that Jesus has given us a magnificent and perfect tool to accomplish it.

Communion: this incredible, masterful, divine gift, is the culture God ordained to transform the difficult processes of sanctification into imminently doable reality! Once understood and experienced in all of its fullness, the Lord's Table becomes a journey that cannot be forgotten or ignored, because the child of God is called to its participation regularly. Even if those who have experienced this kind of ceremony find themselves in another city, or on another side of the world, they will never be able to escape the love to embrace nor the admonitions to consider this ceremony always calls them to. Communion embodies the ideal of the believer and their God, face-to-face, experiencing grace

Michael Wolff

and embracing the true call for confronting cover-ups with other sinners like no other process.

This is holy pressure lived out periodically for the maintenance of our faith. If her instructions are followed, Communion can attack the curses of superficiality and self-deception that marked the Laodicean church, and now cause the *weakness, sickness, and sleep* that mark the church in America. Yet, as with all things given from a loving God, it comes with choice to a people of free will, and a price that must be paid for the rewards. So what will it be?

Dietrich Bonhoeffer so impressed his Nazi prison guards, that they risk their own lives to set up a network to smuggle his writings out of Hitler's death-camp at Flossenberg. He created a community of believers in the most hideous and prosecutorial environment imaginable, and did it in a way that confounded his captors. He wrote this shortly before his death at their hands, just two days before the camp was liberated by the Allies, in his treatise on Christian community: *Life Together:*

> The day of the Lord's Supper is an occasion of joy for [God's] community. Reconciled in their hearts with God and the brethren...[the congregation] is given new fellowship with God and men. Thefellowship of the Lord's Supper is the superlative fulfillment of [the] fellowship...Here the community has reached its goal. Here joy in Christ and His community is complete. The life of the Christian community under the Word has reached its perfection in the sacrament. 51

This spiking event—this exclamation point—this ancient path of house-to-house fellowship much more than mere association, so full of conviction and the power to heal, will take you and your small-group fellowship places you have never been before. It will come slowly, and certainly not without its share of difficulties. It

> **Press on, endure, and get ready for that "new thing" God is always doing.**

will mean radical change in thinking and practice, and that is something people always fear. Yet isn't radical change what we need, in order to engender in the American church the passion and urgency we see in Jesus during His Passover?

Press on, endure, and get ready for that *new thing* God is always doing. It will open doors to closer fellowship, along with numerous opportunities for evangelism and discipleship. I believe it can radically alter the depth of fellowship for any body of believers willing to step out in faith, and just do it. A final visit to the laws of the 12-step is in order here:

> Having had a spiritual awakening as the result of these steps, we tried to carry this message to addicts, and to practice these principles in all our affairs. 52

I sincerely hope that, having had a spiritual awakening to the awesome power of Communion, you will try to carry this message to other sinners, and to practice these principles every time you partake of the Lord's Table. God has given you the ceremony for leading your brothers and sisters back home to true fellowship, and from the dangers of unresolved sin patterns.

When you think about it, evangelists are nothing more than people who have become profoundly changed by some revelation of God in their lives, and then want to share that revelation with others. For the sake of the church, I hope you will become an evangelist for *The Lost Supper*. What do you have to lose? Take a chance on spreading the word, and take your small-group fellowship, and perhaps your church, to the next level!

ATTACHMENTS:

Communion/12-Step Comparison

1. We admitted we were powerless over alcohol - that our lives had become unmanageable. *[We were dead in our trespasses and sins (Eph. 2:1), and realize Jesus is the only way to be forgiven (Eph. 1:7). We have no power over sin apart from this truth]*.

2. Came to believe that a Power greater than ourselves could restore us to sanity. *[If we use the Communion Table the way it was m1 eant, we are restored to sanity from the insanity that self-deception and rationalization of sin causes (Matt. 6:23, 2 Cor. 10:5)]*.

3. 3. Made a decision to turn our will and our lives over to the care of God as we understood Him. *[At the Communion Table we symbolically eat His body and drink His blood, thereby turning ourselves over to His care (John 6:53-56)]*.

4. Made a searching and fearless moral inventory of ourselves. *[We are to examine ourselves, and so eat and drink (1 Cor. 11:27-28)]*

5. Admitted to God, to ourselves and to another human being the exact nature of our wrongs. *[Confession not just vertically (1 Cor. 4:4), but horizontally as well, keeping a clear conscience both before God and men (Acts 24:16), and brings healing (Jas. 5:16)]*.

6. Were entirely ready to have God remove all these defects of character. *[Not having a hard heart towards changes that are needed (Jas. 1:5-8, Luke 18:13-14)]*.

7. Humbly asked Him to remove our shortcomings. *[Time of vertical*

confession (1 Jhn. 1:9, 2 Cor. 12:8-9)].

8. Made a list of all persons we had harmed, and became willing to make amends to them all. *[Communion action: Matthew 5 Alternative (Matt. 5:23-24, Prov. 6:1-5)].*

9. Made direct amends to such people wherever possible, except when to do so would injure them or others. *[Ditto rule #8].*

10. Continued to take personal inventory and when we were wrong promptly admitted it. *[The maintenance of our faith, and why we are told to partake regularly (1 Cor. 11:26, Acts 2:42)].*

11. Sought through prayer and meditation to improve our conscious contact with God as we understood Him, praying only for knowledge of His will for us and the power to carry that out. *[Why we are to "abide in Christ" (John 15:5, 2 Cor. 10:5)].*

12. Having had a spiritual awakening as the result of these steps, we tried to carry this message to alcoholics and to practice these principles in all our affairs. *[Why we are to "bear fruit" by properly partaking and administrating the Table. We need to be biblical Communion "evangelists" to all sinners in the house of God, making true disciples through the proper observation of God's holiest of all ceremonies (Matt. 28:19-20)].*

LEADERSHIP TEACHING/PREPARATION OUTLINE

To administrators of the Table:

Be certain you are prepared, passionate, and have established credibility with your flock through your loving service to them. Review chapters for Bible references as needed, and insert them into the outline. *The Lost Supper* will be a radical departure from what most are used to. They will be resistant to change, and you will be asking them to push their faith in Christ and trust in the fellowship to extents most have rarely experienced. Your love, ability, knowledge, conviction, and passion is what will help them through it.

You hold in your hand the power of the most magnificent gift God ever gave for emotional and spiritual healing. He can use you to destroy the accursed cover-ups that are now paralyzing many of the faithful. If you fail in your responsibilities as a leader, the cover-ups will not only continue, they will be reinforced by a false grace. I am available through my website [www.thereconnectedchurch.org] to help you in whatever way I can. Have the courage to stand up against the status-quo, prepare well, lead and teach well, trust in God, love your flock, and you will do well.

I. Establish the biblical environment

    a. Passover of Exodus: Families gathered in small groups behind closed doors

    b. Jesus' Passover: Preached daily in Temple, but gathered with His spiritual family behind closed doors

        i. Discuss spiritual family per Matt. 12:36-50

    c. The Pentecostal church: broke bread "house to house" while gathering in the Temple for services

II. Why small group environment with plenty of time?

   a. Conducive to embracing the love and considering the admonishments of the Spirit

      i. Review Jesus' balanced message of love and admonishment (John 13-18), and Paul's (1 Cor. 11 Communion instruction)

         1. It's not about grace alone!

   b. People won't open up in large groups full of strangers

      i. Trust built through small groups best for transparency

   c. It takes time to teach properly, and to engage in individual prayer and small group confessional

III. Discuss warnings to believers and unbelievers in Paul's instructions

   a. Unbelievers: 1 Cor. 11:23-26 – Must be able to proclaim Jesus' name to participate [make sure they know they are welcome to observe!]

   b. Believers: vs's. 27-31 – Must not come with hard hearts or covered-up sin patterns

      i. Causing the spiritual weakness, sickness, and sleep we see in church today

   c. Here is where we deal with, and break, such patterns

      i. Review foundational areas of sin (per chapter VII)

IV. The Matthew 5 Alternative

   a. This is where we will "here remember" what God or our brother has against us if we will be open to a thorough self-exam before God and man

- b. What to do if kingdom business needs to be tended to
  - i. Leave our offering at the Altar [abstain], go take care of business, and return in victory!
    1. Review the responsibilities of the fellowship concerning follow up
- c. The only sin at the Table is taking unworthily, not abstinence [unless that done to ignore responsibilities to confront and confess]
  - i. Encourage abstinence and participation as *both* being victories if done in interest of becoming real
- d. Why Communion given to us as a regular ceremony: to keep dealing with our sinful state and ongoing abilities to rationalize and cover-up
- e. Review step 9-10 of the 12-step program

V. Individual prayer, and corporate confession and prayer

- a. Individual prayer: Time to open souls to God's conviction
  - i. Not time for intercession for others, but deliberate opening to examination by the Spirit to discern what He or others "may have against us"
  - ii. Make copies of prayer recorder at end of book, and ask participants to review verses there before going to prayer
    1. Encourage them to record everything the Spirit brings to mind. If they won't, cover-ups are indicated
  - iii. Review step 1-4, 6-7, 11 of 12-step program [using "sin" instead of "alcohol," and "Jesus" instead of "God as we knew him"]
- b. Corporate confession and prayer: Stress uniqueness of James 5:16
  - i. Forgiveness through vertical confession, healing through

horizontal

    1. Must at least begin to confront issues on prayer recorder or admit rationalizing and denial

        a. If people can't confront encourage abstinence

    2. God will not heal if we refuse to confess to others

  ii. Review steps 5, 8 of the 12-step program

VI. Miscellaneous other teachings [best done in prior studies in interest of time, and retention abilities of your flock]

  a. The Soma: are we aiding the body in its journey or holding it back?

  b. What to do in corporate settings when warnings not given

  c. Prodigal Son analogy

VII. Logistics for powerful ceremony

  a. Best in groups of men, women, or youth [boys and girls together]

    i. Men and women together not best, but can split them up during confessional time if necessary

  b. Getaway place with no distractions: Like Jesus did

    i. Not at a place owned by someone in the group

    ii. Overnight a great environment

    iii. Have people travel in groups and perhaps eat a meal on the way to stimulate fellowship

    iv. One cell phone or pager only for emergencies

  c. Use other small groups to reciprocate child care [don't bring children of any age]

  d. Open with prayer and worship

i. Bring worship leader if possible to set tone

      1. Simple songs with large print song sheets [nothing complicated]

   e. Always and in every situation teach basics

      i. Transparency before God and men

      ii. Warnings of 1 Cor. 11

      iii. Review typical sin foundations and patterns

      iv. Matthew 5 Alternative

      v. Importance of individual prayer time *and* corporate confession

      vi. Abstinence or participation

   f. Partaking of the Elements

      i. Final review of importance of being real with God

         1. Abstinence and participation *both* victories if done with right heart

         2. Solemnly warn any from eating and drinking judgment upon themselves if they know they have kingdom business to attend to and are ignoring it

   g. Importance of the accountability, assistance, and prayer of the fellowship for return of those struggling in victory

PRAYER RECORDER

Heb. 4:12-13: "For the word of God is living and active and sharper than any two-edged sword, and piercing as far as the division of soul and spirit…and able to judge the thoughts and intentions of the heart… All things are open and laid bare to the eyes of Him…"

Ps. 139:23-24: "Search me, O God, and know my heart; try me and know my anxious thoughts; and see if there be any hurtful way in me."

Prov. 15:11, "Sheol and Abaddon lie open before the Lord, how much more the hearts of men!"

1 Cor. 4:4-5: "The one who examines me is the Lord…wait until the Lord comes, who will both bring to light the things hidden in the darkness, and disclose the motives of men's hearts."

Ps. 90:8: "You have placed our iniquities before You; our secret sins in the light of Your presence."

A love I need to embrace: _____
_____
_____
_____
_____
_____
_____
_____
_____

Admonishments I need to consider: _____
_____
_____
_____

_____
_____
_____
_____

Cover-ups and sinful practices I've not confessed:_____
_____
_____
_____
_____
_____
_____
_____
_____

I need to "go quickly" and...(Matthew 5): _____
_____
_____
_____
_____
_____
_____

Encouragement/admonishment for another: _____
_____
_____
_____
_____
_____
_____

[Use back side of this form if needed]

ACKNOWLEDGMENTS

13. Robert Lewis, Raising a Modern Day Knight, page 100, ISBN-10: 1589973097, ISBN-13:978-1589973091
14. Dr. Larry Crabb, Connecting, page 97, ISBN-10: 0849945291, ISBN-13: 978-0849945298
15. Rocky Mountain News, ©February 26, 2004
16. Dietrich Bonhoeffer, Life Together, page 107, ISBN-10: 0060608528, ISBN-13: 978-0060608521
17. Michael Wells, Lifelines Newsletter, ©02/08, Abiding Life Press
18. Eugene Peterson, The Message, page 347, ISBN-10: 1576835197, ISBN-13: 978-1576835197
19. Oswald Chambers, My Utmost for His Highest, no page, ISBN-10:1602601860 , ISBN-13: 978-1602601864
20. Abiding Life Press, ©2005, no page
21. Ibid #4, pages 22-23
22. Ibid #2, page 82
23. Ibid #7, no page
24. Steps 1 & 3, Alcoholics Anonymous Twelve-Step Program
25. Rob Bell, Velvet Elvis, page 59, ISBN-10: 0310273080, ISBN-13: 978-0310273080
26. Ibid #6, page 657
27. Louis Berkhof, Systematic Theology, page 657, ISBN-10:0802838200 , ISBN-13: 978-0802838200
28. Lawrence Kimbrough-Ray Pritchard, Men of Character, no page, ISBN-10: 080542685X, ISBN-13: 978-0805426854
29. Ibid #4, page 116
30. Ibid #2, pages 86, 91
31. Excerpts from the Trip Report—Nepal, ©02/03, Abiding Life Press , page 1
32. Lifelines Newsletter, ©02/08, Abiding Life Press
33. Beyond Renewal, Brian Hathaway, page 80-81, ISBN-10: 0850093392, ISBN-13: 978-0850093391
34. John Eldrege, Wild at Heart, page 142, ISBN-10: 0785287965, ISBN-13: 978-0785287964
35. Matthew Henry's Commentary from PC Study Bible, ©1995, Biblesoft

36. Ibid #7, no page
37. Matthew Henry's Commentary, ISBN-10: 1598562754, ISBN-13: 978-1598562750
38. Ibid #15, page 656
39. Steps 8 & 9, Alcoholics Anonymous Twelve-Step Program
40. Ibid #16, no page
41. Ibid #23
42. Martin Luther: public domain
43. Step 5, Alcoholics Anonymous Twelve-Step Program
44. Ibid # 4, page 112
45. Ibid #4, page 27
46. Ibid #4, page 105
47. Ibid #4, page 104
48. Lifelines Newsletter, ©11/08, Abiding Life Press
49. Ibid #2, page 98
50. Michael Wells, 2008 Trip Report
51. Steps 11& 8, Alcoholics Anonymous Twelve-Step Program
52. Step 5, Alcoholics Anonymous Twelve-Step Program
53. Ibid #4, page 116
54. Ibid #13, page 110
55. Steps 6, 8, 9, Alcoholics Anonymous Twelve-Step Program
56. Rick Rusaw and Eric Swanson, The Externally Focused Church, page.112, ISBN-10: 0764427404, ISBN-13: 978-0764427404
57. Ibid #7, no page
58. Ibid #21, page 21
59. Erdman's Handbook to the Bible, page 154, ASIN: B000GSKPLK
60. Ibid #13, page 171
61. Step 10, Alcoholics Anonymous Twelve-Step Program
62. Dietrich Bonhoeffer, The Cost of Discipleship, page 59, ASIN: B0017LNTR2
63. Ibid #4, page 122
64. Step 12, Alcoholics Anonymous Twelve-Step Program

www.ingramcontent.com/pod-product-compliance
Lightning Source LLC
Chambersburg PA
CBHW021406060725
29181CB00036B/105